How Can I Wake Up When I Don't Know I'm Asleep?

Selected Essays By

Ted Kuntz

Author, Peace Begins With Me

Published in Canada
Copyright 2015 by Ted Kuntz
201–3041 Anson Ave. Coquitlam
British Columbia, Canada V3B 2H6
First printing – July 2015

**How Can I Wake Up
When I Don't Know I'm Asleep / Ted Kuntz**

ISBN 9781514197882

1. Inspirational 2. Self-improvement

Cover photo by Karl Hermann Photography.

Cover: INUKSHUK, English Bay, Vancouver.
Inukshuk - Monuments made of unworked stones that are
used by the Inuit for communication and survival. The
traditional meaning of the inukshuk is *"Someone was here"* or
"You are on the right path."

Essays

Opening Thoughts

Since writing **Peace Begins With Me** in 2005 I have been asked if I'm planning to write another book. I've had the intention to write again for many years, however I was challenged because I didn't know what the content would be. All I knew was the title - *'How Can I Wake Up When I Don't Know I'm Asleep?'*

I've recognized for a long time that humanity needs to wake up. This knowing has sat in my bones and interrupted my sleep. Then a number of years ago I was invited to become a regular contributor to a local newspaper. On a monthly basis I would summon my courage and share my thoughts and reflections with my fellow neighbors and friends.

My reflections and writings were not always gentle. I admit there was often an edge to my writings. In hindsight I recognize this was my way of prodding and poking my fellow citizens to wake up.

My belief is humanity needs to wake up. The need to wake up is not simply on the level of desire. It is a necessity. Humanity, more often than not, behaves in unconscious and destructive ways that cause harm to each other and to this beautiful planet. This destruction needs to stop.

This will not be an easy book to read. You will be tested, poked, prodded and stretched. I intend to push you out of your comfort zone and beyond your current state of consciousness. I'm a proponent of Einstein's message that *"insanity is doing the same and expecting a different outcome"*.

My goal is to invite, encourage, and insist that we **all** do something different.

In my experience the solutions often exist outside of our current frame of reference or our current way of thinking. We need to step outside of the box of our programming and open to bigger, broader and different ways of thinking.

I know many of you will be challenged by some, possibly most of the essays I've written. Let me be clear. This is my intention – to expand and stretch your way of thinking. I am intentionally being provocative. I am intentionally inviting you to look at something *you think you already know* and consider it *again* from a different perspective.

When confronted with new or different perspectives our tendency is to dismiss, label, judge and discount what we experience as different. Author Ray Woollam calls this *"binning"* - the act of sticking an idea or perspective into a bin labeled 'right' or 'wrong', 'good' or 'bad'.

I'm hoping you won't do that. I invite you to sit in the confusion and disorientation that a different perspective offers. My wish is that you respond with *curiosity*, *consideration*, and a *desire* to deepen your understanding. Then, from a deeper understanding, choose again.

I've intentionally chosen the title – **How Can I Wake Up When I Don't Know I'm Asleep**. Most of us are unaware that we are asleep and living in unconscious and programmed ways. We assume that what we have been told by our teachers, religious leaders, governments, and medical authorities is true. We tend to be *compliant* rather than *curious*, and fail to fully investigate and discern truth for ourselves.

6

I invite you to set aside your programming, put down the remote, and sit in the space of not knowing for a few hours. Resist either *agreeing* or *disagreeing* with me. Resist *labeling* or *judging*. Please just *consider* and allow your inner wisdom to guide you to your truth.

Many of the essays were inspired by the news events of the day - personal, local, national and international. What follows is sixty-seven of the essays and reflections penned over a ten-year period. While some of the essays are dated and about a particular time and place, the themes and questions are timeless and transcend the actual event.

It is my genuine hope these reflections will be of service to you and bring you closer to what we are all capable of becoming – loving, peaceful, and conscious beings.

Namaste

Ted Kuntz

Binning is a colossal avoidance of the
human capacities to accept difference, to consider,
to think, to choose,
to understand, or to learn.

Binning will not change the situation,
but it will change me in a manner that renders me tense,
frustrated, or ineffective.

~ Ray Woollam, Author
On Choosing With A Quiet Mind

The Struggle to Wake Up

We need to wake up! We need to step out of the insanity we regularly dwell in. Eckhart Tolle (**A New Earth**, 2005) speaks of the insanity of the human condition. He states - *"If one needs evidence of the world's insanity, just open a newspaper or turn on the news."* The level of unconsciousness of the human condition is unfortunately all too evident.

Last week I did just that. I turned on my computer and invited Google to share with me the news of the day. This is a small sampling of what humanity was engaged in on March 1, 2012:

   - Elections Canada is attempting to identify the perpetrator in the 'robo-call scandal' in Ottawa. This is a scheme where voters were intentionally misdirected to non-existent voting stations.

   - The world's leading scientists criticize the Canadian Government for preventing scientists from speaking publicly about their research findings.

   - Israel is looking for support to initiate a unilateral, pre-emptive military strike on Iran.

   - A presidential candidate in the United States announces that building the Keystone pipeline from Alberta to Texas is "a no-brainer".

   - The Canadian government has committed to purchasing a number of stealth fighter jets costing hundreds of millions of dollars each.

I could go on but I think the point is clear. The on-going amount of aggression, destruction, deception and greed is deeply disturbing. Why is it we fail to understand the impact of our behavior on both a personal and global level? What enables us to literally cut down the last tree, harvest the last fish, build another oil pipeline, or initiate another war? Is not the insanity of these behaviors abundantly clear for all to see?

I appreciate there is a tendency to glorify the North American First Nations people prior to their contact with the white man. The First Nations people, however, understood something we don't seem to understand. They knew the importance of living in harmony with Nature. They respected the wisdom and life experience of their elders. They honored all life and took only what was necessary to sustain life. They made decisions with the long-range perspective of how a decision might impact the next seven generations. Archeological evidence verifies Native people lived this way for more than ten thousand years before the arrival of the first Europeans.

In the last few hundred years we have caused so much destruction that we are at risk of immense global destruction. How did we become so disconnected from the Earth and from other species? How did we fall into such a deep sleep of unconsciousness that we are able to behave in these destructive ways and not see the error in this way of living?

Sometimes I get mired in my despair. At other times I trust there is value in this experience. I've learned there is value in struggle. My own journey of making peace with my son's disabilities enabled me to live a far richer and more meaningful life than the one prior to Josh becoming disabled.

I've acquired beautiful wisdom about peace, joy, acceptance and forgiveness. I've come to a deeper appreciation of what is truly important in life.

I'm not sure I would have learned these lessons without the deep suffering Josh's disability caused and my commitment to making peace with his condition.

In the same way I hope our current crises - environmental, political, economic and moral will deepen us collectively and enable us to achieve a higher state of consciousness. It is my hope that the depth of our crises is a reflection of the depth of the wisdom we can attain.

In my work as a Psychotherapist I often ask, *"What is the gift in this struggle that is before you?"* Initially the question is difficult for most to embrace. Individuals are so impacted by their suffering they are unable to consider that any benefit could result from their struggle. I've regularly witnessed that as individuals successfully move through their struggle and emerge out the other side, the gifts and benefits of the difficult journey are revealed.

It is my hope there are many gifts in humanity's current struggle; that these gifts might include a higher state of consciousness; a deeper compassion for the human condition regardless of race, culture, religion, nation, gender or ability; a richer understanding of our inter-connectedness with all species on the planet; and a deeper respect and gratitude for life.

It is my hope that we are on a journey of awakening to the Divine beings that we are!

Unless we change our direction,
we will end up where we are headed.

~ Chinese Saying

How Are The Children?

A number of life altering decisions are before us. These decisions are being made around the boardrooms and caucus tables of various government and non-government organizations around the world.

Discussions are occurring in the White House of the United States government, the halls of Canada's Parliament Building, the offices of the National Energy Board, and various meeting rooms of environmental groups, citizen advocacy organizations and First Nations Councils.

Many will not describe the decisions as "*life altering*". Most of the dialogue will be about *"financial benefit"* and *"economic development"*. To frame the conversation in the language of life altering is a perspective many will resist.

The decisions I'm referring to are the multiple proposals for consideration including: the twinning of the Kinder Morgan Trans Mountain Pipeline, the Keystone XL Pipeline, the Northern Gateway Extension, the Athabasca Pipeline Twinning Project, among others. What each of these initiatives has in common is a significant expansion of the extraction of bitumen from the Alberta Tar Sands.

Proponents of the pipelines and tar sands extraction would have us believe these actions are the only reasonable actions given our dependence upon oil and oil products. Defenders of the Keystone XL pipeline argue that not building the pipeline will not reduce world-wide carbon emissions because some one else will built a pipeline and the carbon will be released anyways.

The idea of leaving the bitumen in the ground is not, in their view, a viable option.

There are all kinds of economic arguments that make pipeline development the right choice. And if economics were the only criteria for success the decision would be an easy one. However economics is but one consideration, and I would argue the least important consideration. If a hierarchy of needs were established similar to Maslow's hierarchy of needs, **life** would always come before **money**.

We are beyond speculation on the effects of carbon emissions on global warming and climate change. There is increasing evidence that our carbon-based economy is eroding the very livability of the planet. Elizabeth Kolbert, author of the powerful book, <u>**The Sixth Extinction**</u> (2014), asserts that we are witnessing a wide-scale dying off of species comparable to five earlier extinction events.

The culprit behind this extinction is not an asteroid, but rather a single species - human beings.

In countless ways we are rendering the Earth uninhabitable to many of our fellow Earth-dwellers.

Kolbert states: *"It is estimated that one-third of all reef-building corals, a third of all freshwater mollusks, a third of sharks and rays, a quarter of all mammals, a fifth of all reptiles, and a sixth of all birds are headed toward oblivion."*

We need to use our intelligence, one of humanity's greatest gifts, to figure out how to live in peace with our fellow creatures. The violence that humans have done to the planet will not heal without a change in direction. Countless species have already died or are doomed.

There is a Chinese saying that states: *"Unless we change our direction, we will end up where we are headed."* The direction we are headed is becoming increasingly dire, such that to say "yes" to any of the decisions before our governments and National Energy Board is akin to mass insanity.

The Maasai people of Africa, one of the most respected tribes on the African continent, offer this daily greeting to each other: *"How are the children?"* The traditional response is, *"The children are well."* If we were honest with ourselves we would need to respond with, *"The children are in danger."*

Will we sit passively and allow our governments and corporations to make decisions that are not life sustaining? Will we continue to indulge in practices that encourage and support tar sands extraction? Will we do more of the same and expect a different outcome?

Ultimately the decision belongs to each and every one of us. The future of our children and grandchildren is in our hands.

He who tells the stories
rules the world.

~ Hopi Saying

The Value of Storytelling

The people of the Hopi First Nations understood the power of stories. They had a strong oral tradition and used storytelling as the means to transfer wisdom from one generation to the next. Carefully embedded within each story were the values, skills and knowledge the elders deemed necessary to navigate the challenges of life successfully.

In my journey to create peace and joy in my life I too have come to recognize the power of stories - both the stories I tell myself, and the stories I allow to be told to me. I've learned that by carefully managing the stories in my life I can create the experience of peace and joy. The secret to living joyfully is to recognize one's role as a *storyteller* and to take full responsibility for the stories I tell myself and allow to be told to me.

A number of years ago I came across an article in a parent magazine. The title of the article was - **Who Tells the Stories**

Our Children Hear? The author, Michael Warren, explained the power of storytelling and reminded parents that it was common for parents and grandparents to sit with a child and tell them a story. The act of storytelling was both an act of intimacy and an opportunity to teach something valuable to the child.

Warren then asked the question - *"Who is the primary storyteller of children today?"* For most the answer is obvious - the television and the computer.

The problem, Warren explains, is we have given away the responsibility for storytelling to people we don't know and who often don't share our values. Warren implores parents to take back the responsibility of story telling.

What is meant by '*storytelling*'? The fact is that in our efforts to understand this complex world we are given short cuts as a way of filtering information and determining what needs to be paid attention to and what is irrelevant. Stories are a way of making sense of the world. We are constantly presented with stories about who is good and who is not, what is safe and unsafe, what is important and unimportant, and who is to be believed and who is not to be believed.

When I was a child I was told stories about who was going to Heaven and who was going to Hell. Those who shared the same religion as I were guaranteed a spot in Heaven, while the others, no matter how well intended or kind were destined for Hell. Today the stories have more to do with who is good and who is evil. Any one who is on the side of democracy or capitalism is good, while those who live in the Middle East or have a different form of government are evil.

If one were to simply accept the stories delivered via the major media one would spend much of their time living in fear of the number of terrorists who have suddenly arisen in the last decade. Witness the justification to manufacture thousands of fighter jets and drones, build permanent military bases through out the world, and declare endless wars. The truth is *'terrorism'* is just a story. We are twice as likely to die from a peanut allergy then at the hands of a terrorist.

I believe we are wise to be more discerning about the stories we tell our self and those we allow to be told to us. By far the majority of humans are not dangerous or evil. My firsthand experience informs me most individuals are kind, considerate and loving. I've experienced over and over again the love, generosity and kindness of others.

Many years ago I unplugged my television because the stories it offered did not reflect the world I know. I unsubscribed to my national newspaper and I permitted my own first hand experience to be more credible and valid than the stories that were being told via the mass media.

Many individuals fear they will become *uniformed* if they dare to disconnect from the mass media storytellers. I remind them of the words of Mark Twain –

"If you don't read the newspapers, you are uninformed. If you do read the newspapers, you are misinformed."

We might be wise to adopt the advice of Albert Einstein who stated –

"If you want your children to be intelligent, tell them fairy tales."

There is no coming to consciousness without pain.
People will do anything, no matter how absurd,
in order to avoid facing their own Soul.

One does not become enlightened
by imagining figures of light,
but by making the darkness conscious.

~ C.G. Jung

The Challenge to Be Relevant

Many years ago Richard Dal Monte, editor of the **Tri City News**, invited me to become a regular contributor to The News. I experienced many thoughts and emotions in considering how to respond to Mr. Dal Monte's request.

One response was delight in being offered the opportunity to contribute to the collective consciousness of my community. I believe the media serves a critical role in forming and deepening the understanding and attitudes of a community.

A second response was disbelief. I thought it ironic that I was being asked to participate as a member of the media. I have not been very complimentary of the media.

I'm of the opinion that most of the media today does a grave disservice to the community by raising issues out of proportion to their true significance, by heightening fear and anxiety, by creating divisions between aspects of community and creating polarities that negate the underlying unity between people, and by over simplifying issues.

I wondered, if I accepted Mr. Dal Monte's invitation, would I become complicit in this disservice in some way?

Then I viewed the movie **Good Night and Good Luck** (2005), a documentary that captured the courage and vision of Edward R. Murrow. Murrow was the news director for CBS television during the McCarthy era.

Murrow distinguished himself by using television to thoughtfully, respectfully and courageously challenge Senator McCarthy during a time when many were intimidated into silence by the McCarthy investigation.

The film opened with Murrow being honored by the Television Broadcasters Association of America for his role in giving America back its voice. In his response to their tribute Murrow challenged his media colleagues to become *"relevant"*.

Murrow was of the opinion that the media, even then, had degenerated into focusing solely on *entertaining* and *simplifying* rather than using their power to raise the community to a higher standard of collective living. Murrow's message impacted me.

A Nation of sheep
soon begets a government
of wolves.
~ Edward R. Murrow

I decided to accept Mr. Dal Monte's offer. I decided to use the opportunity as a platform to share ideas in a way that might facilitate *reflection* rather than *reaction*, to use this invitation to *deepen* our collective understanding, both mine and the reader's, of current issues and affairs, and to express the *hopes*, *dreams* and *values* of my neighbors.

It is my hope that I have assisted in some small way to transcend the tendency to divide citizens into 'us' and 'them', 'for' and 'against', 'right' and 'wrong'.

Sam Sullivan, the Mayor of Vancouver, when asked his opinion on a contentious civic matter replied, *"The perception is that the decision is between the right and wrong answer on this matter.*
In truth there is no right or wrong answer, only different perspectives on what is important."

I desire to be an agent who helps to *illuminate* what is important, someone who *unites* a community around shared values and ideals, and a person who *invites* and *creates* opportunities for reflection and dialogue.

I hope to raise more *questions* than answers, to create more *curiosity* than certainty, and more *discussion* and debate than simplicity.

I'm grateful for this opportunity to participate in our growing consciousness of our community and hope I serve us all well.

I cannot think myself into a new way of living.
I have to live myself into a new way of thinking.

~ Claude Thomas, Buddhist monk

Creating This Human Experience

The beginning of a New Year is an opportunity to re-commit and re-imagine the experiences and intentions one wishes to set for the coming year. Most declare one or more personal goals as the focus of their intentions - weight loss, increased saving, more family or couple time, better health, etc.

The New Year is a good time to also declare one's intentions for the larger human experience. The fact is each of us collectively participates in co-creating our community experience both locally and nationally. The state of the human condition at this time demands that we lift our attention from our individual, family-centric perspective and expand our view to include a larger sphere.

When we broaden our perspective to a larger field of endeavor it is easy to become intimidated with the largeness of a situation and perceive ourselves as small and insignificant. It is also common to become overwhelmed with the severity of a situation and move into a state of despair.

Neither condition will serve us. More than ever our voices, efforts and perspectives are needed to claim and create the kind of human conditions we endeavor to achieve.

My invitation to you is to select *one* area of focus - environmental stewardship, social justice, poverty reduction, harm reduction, inclusion, civil rights, etc. and align yourself with like-minded souls.

More than ever we need thoughtful and dedicated people *consciously* creating the human experience where everyone can thrive.

In 1940 Charlie Chaplin directed a movie entitled **The Great Dictator**. Chaplin's movie was an effort to unite men in a common cause for the betterment of all humanity. His words were not heeded then. Maybe we will heed them now.

> *"We all want to help one another. Human beings are like that. We want to live by each other's happiness, not by each other's misery. We don't want to hate and despise one another. In this world there is room for everyone. And the good earth is rich and can provide for everyone. The way of life can be free and beautiful, but we have lost the way.*
>
> *Greed has poisoned men's souls; has barricaded the world with hate; has goose-stepped us into misery and bloodshed. We have developed speed, but we have shut ourselves in. Machinery that gives abundance has left us in want. Our knowledge has made us cynical; our cleverness, hard and unkind.*
>
> *We think too much and feel too little. More than machinery, we need humanity. More than cleverness, we need kindness and gentleness. Without these qualities, life will be violent and all will be lost.*
>
> *Let us all unite. Let us fight for a new world, a decent world that will give men a chance to work, that will give youth a future and old age a security. By the promise of these things, brutes have risen to power. But they lie! They do not fulfill their promise.*

Now let us fight to fulfill that promise! Let us fight to free the world! To do away with national barriers! To do away with greed, with hate and intolerance!

Let us fight for a world of reason, a world where science and progress will lead to all men's happiness."

My own personal initiative is to support an emerging movement entitled **World Beyond War** (www.worldbeyondwar.org). I just signed their declaration of peace and will endeavor to use my time and talents to raise the potential of mankind to affirm a world beyond warfare.

My hope is you find your cause and your voice and the human condition becomes kinder, gentler and more loving for all.

Who is man?
What is his purpose?
What is life?
What is good?
What is evil?
Who decides?

~ Edward Tell

Don't Make Me Think For Myself

For the first time in history individuals are being encouraged to make their own decisions. Previously we lived under a hierarchical structure where a small group of religious and political leaders made decisions for us. Even in industry it was common for a small group of people to identify priorities and solutions and communicate these decisions to the rank and file to be acted on. Leadership was the responsibility of the few. Now we are being asked to share the responsibilities of leadership and to think for ourselves.

I remember the first time I was required to think for myself. It was in high school in a Grade 11 English class. At the start of the semester our teacher, Mr. Edward Tell, outlined the requirements for the coming term. The final essay, he explained, would be one question - "*What is man?*" The entire course will be devoted to developing an answer to this broad philosophical question.

We would be reading various works of English literature that considered the human condition. Books as **Finnegan's Wake** by James Joyce, and **Heart of Darkness** by Joseph Conrad were assigned reading. Each lecture was a series of questions - one more deep and penetrating than the last. Questions as - "*Who is man? What is his purpose? What is life? What is good? What is evil? Who decides?*"

I studiously copied all of the questions into my notebook. I anticipated that at some point Mr. Tell would provide the answers for us to copy into our notebooks as well. Much to my dismay the questions continued.

After weeks of relentless questioning without the offering of any sort of answer I finally had had enough. I put up my hand. *"Mr. Tell"*, I asked, *"When are you going to give us the answers to all these questions?"* Mr. Tell laughed. It wasn't his responsibility to answer these questions. It was mine.

Panic and fear washed over me. It was inconceivable that I should be the one to answer these questions. I was lost. I was unprepared for the task of thinking for myself. I knew how to gather information, but I didn't know how to evaluate this information. I was fearful of arriving at the wrong answer. Not wanting to be wrong kept me vigilant to determine what others had agreed were the right answers. Now Mr. Tell was informing me that it was *my* responsibility to decide. I panicked at the thought that I would need to figure this out for myself.

In hindsight I see now how I had spent most of my life looking to others for the answers to life's questions. My assumption was that others knew better than I did. My own ability to consider, reflect, discern and decide was undeveloped. Up until that point in my life my role had been to take the answers and the direction of others and follow them as carefully and conscientiously as I could.

This shift from wisdom being *'externally determined'* to becoming *'internally determined'* is a shift that all of us are being asked to make. We are all being challenged to take responsibility for our life, for our choices, and for our actions.

It is being demanded of us to share in the responsibility of sorting out life's questions and challenges. While this responsibility may feel like a burden, in truth this is our liberation. When we finally embrace our capacity and our right to choose we step into our *freedom* and *power*.

Now I am of the understanding that the goal of life is to claim our power and to assume a leadership role. Only when we all come from a place of leadership and personal responsibility will we live rich and meaningful lives in harmony with one another.

It is up to each of us to define what is important and to define our purpose in life. Life is about answering the question, "*Who am I?*" "*Who will I choose to be in this moment?*" Life is a series of choices.

When a challenge is before me I now ask, "*What would I like to accomplish? What does success look like to me?*" When faced with adversity I've learned to ask, "*Whom will I choose to be in this moment? What action of mine will do the most good?*" These are questions that no one else can answer for me.

I have finally embraced my responsibility to live as a *creative* being rather than a *reactive* being. A creative being is one who chooses with intention and who acts knowing that they have the power to create their experience.

Healthy families, healthy organizations and healthy communities are ones that encourage *all* members to accept their responsibility to choose and to act. To excel in this world we must embrace our responsibility for leadership, not *over* others, but over oneself.

We are being offered an opportunity to enter a new reality - a reality of our choosing.

*Out beyond ideas of wrong doing
and right doing there is a field.
I'll meet you there.*

~ Rumi

Beyond Black and White

Life would be simple if everything were black or white, good or bad, right or wrong. It would make decision-making much easier. Life, however, isn't this simple. Life is a rich tapestry of competing demands that require each of us to weigh the advantages and disadvantages of a number of possibilities, anticipate their impact both short and long term, and then choose.

And so when one looks at the world through the lens of *black/white, right/wrong, good/bad, and victim/villain* they do a disservice, not only to others, but to one self as well. I deprive myself of the opportunity to deepen my understanding of an issue or individual when my perception is overly simple and superficial.

I regularly witness this over simplification of reality in the reporting of events like war. I notice how the language used is often simple and polarized: *freedom fighters vs. insurgents, coalition forces vs. terrorists, heroes vs. villains, good guys vs. bad guys.*

It is not just with issues of war where black/white thinking is imposed upon us. Consider medical decisions where labels as *'pro-vaccine'* or *'anti-vaccine'* are utilized. And discussions where those with differing perspectives are rigidly identified as either *'environmentalists'* or *'capitalists'*, as if we are only one aspect.

Politicians are regularly guilty of reducing complex issues to right/wrong, left/right, liberal/conservative labeling. As a result we compress complex reality into small containers rather than engage the richness of life in a respectful dialogue to better understand our modern world.

It pains me to see life treated this way - reduced through the use of words and phrases to a shadow of its true complexity and richness. But I want to draw out a larger issue here. I want to focus on what happens when we see the world through the lens of right/wrong and when we paint others as good/bad.

Ray Woollam has written a number of thought provoking books including, **On Choosing With A Quiet Mind** (1985) and **Have a Plain Day** (1989). Woollam believes many of us spend our entire lives *avoiding* thinking, considering, weighing or choosing. Instead we do what he calls "*binning*".

Woollam observes that most human beings act as if there are only two bins. One bin has the label 'good' written on the side. The other bin is given the label 'bad'. Their entire thinking process is reduced to stuffing life into either of these two bins.

Woollam notices we call these bins by different names - right/wrong, good/bad, left/right, liberal/conservative, but the effect is the same - we diminish life to an over simplified game of "binning".

According to Woollam –

"Binning is a colossal avoidance of the human capacities to accept difference, to consider, to think, to choose, to understand, or to learn. Binning will not change the situation, but it will change me in a manner that renders me tense, frustrated, or ineffective."

The overly simplified judging of others and issues creates an emotional reactivity that prevents and avoids more considered thought. Why investigate a situation further when a decision has already been rendered, when the conclusion has already been reached? Why struggle to understand others who perceive the world different? Simply stick a label on them and move on.

I've spent much of my life 'binning'. As a result I was emotionally reactive. I lived in constant judgment. I saw people as either 'for' what I believed or 'against' what I believed. It took me years of suffering to discover that the source of my suffering was *my way of seeing the world* rather than *the world itself*. This overly simplistic refusal to think, to understand, or to learn is destructive. It hurts everyone involved.

If we truly want to be wise and healthy human beings, if we want to live in peace and harmony with one another, if we want to solve the world's problems, it is essential that we recognize that our way of seeing the world can cause agitation, reactivity and wars rather than compassion, understanding and peace.

We all deserve better. It starts with our willingness to see beyond black and white.

*The style of leadership needed is different
than leadership in the past.
Our challenges today are too complex
to be resolved by a top down style of leadership.*

*What is required is a leadership that demonstrates
courage in the face of adversity,
innovation and creativity in the face of complexity,
and humility and receptivity in the face of difficulty.*

~ Elizabeth Debold
The Business of Saving the World

Moving From Insanity to Sustainability

Author and spiritual teacher Eckhart Tolle writes of
humanity's collective insanity in his 2005 book, **<u>A New Earth</u>**.
Tolle could well be writing about the tar sands development,
Northern Gateway or **Kinder Morgan's Trans Mountain**
pipeline expansion project when he states:

> *"Another aspect of the collective dysfunction*
> *of the human mind*
> *is the unprecedented violence that humans*
> *are inflicting on other life-forms*
> *and the planet itself - the destruction*
> *of oxygen-producing forests*
> *. . . and poisoning of rivers, oceans, and air.*
>
> *Driven by greed, ignorant of their*
> *connectedness to the whole,*
> *humans persist in behavior that, if continued unchecked,*
> *can only result in their own destruction."*

Today is the time to declare our intention. Now is the time to
make a decision to either do *'more of the same'*, or to do
'something different'. Now is the time to consider whether
profits are more important than life.

Below is the submission I provided to the National Energy
Board. I encourage you to make a decision and to take an
action. This decision may be the most important decision of
our lives.

The expansion of pipelines carrying tar sands products increases significantly the investment in oil sands production and ensures an increasing trajectory of oil/bitumen development in Canada. The result will be expanded development of the tar sands, expanded movement of oil products in pipelines, and expanded shipping on our coasts. All of these activities increase the potential for devastating damage to our environment, our commercial fishing, the well being of our coastal communities, and our reliance on tourism.

At some point a decision needs to be made that expanded tar sands development is not the best direction for Canada to pursue. Like the frog in warm water that stays in the water even when it starts to boil, humans are metaphorically immersed in water that is ready to boil. Leadership beyond oil dependency is what is most needed in Canada.

I personally live on False Creek in Vancouver. The high potential exists that increased oil tanker traffic will lead to a catastrophic spill that will damage our waterways for generations. Not only will personal home values be affected, (quite frankly the least of my concerns), but more importantly, the livability of my community for my grand children's children.

We have a decision to make. Will we show leadership in the long term, or succumb to short-term financial benefit at the expense of long-term sustainability? It is not a question of "if" there is a major oil spill. It is a question of "when". The Native people had it right - make decisions based upon seven generations.

I am not willing to increase the risk to our local and global communities and I hope you will not as well. Consideration beyond short-term profits and energy is needed.

Please leave a legacy that we can all be proud of. Canada is blessed with one of the most pristine environments in the world. Let's preserve this gift.

Never doubt that a small group of committed individuals can change the world.
Indeed, it is the only thing that ever does.

~ Margaret Mead

How To Change the World

We are at a crossroads. Some kind of change in direction is needed. More of the same will not save us from our own demise. Radical new ways of thinking and living are needed if we hope to sustain our existence on this planet.

The recent collapse of our economic structures, our deepening destruction of the environment, the erosion of our personal rights and freedoms, our ongoing commitment to armed hostilities both at home and in distant countries means we need to awaken from this insanity. Insanity, as the saying goes, *"is doing more of the same and expecting a different outcome"*.

So how do we change the world? How do we chart a different path? What else can guide us in our pursuit of happiness and success other than consumption and growth?

Like a hamster on a wheel we seem to think the solution is to go faster. But what if going slower is what is needed? What if the solution begins by pausing and reflecting and asking whether the direction we are headed is where we want and need to go? Maybe, as Stephen Covey, author of **Seven Habits of Highly Effective People** (1989) states, we need to pause in our efforts to climb the 'ladder of success' and evaluate whether the ladder is leaning against the right building.

We are not good at pausing, suspending our actions, and reflecting. Many of us are not brave enough to admit that we are lost. Most governments and funding agencies only want to finance the *'doing'* action of an organization. Little thought, energy or resources are dedicated to the *'reflecting'* action that is needed to succeed in a fast changing world.

The world is a different place than it was even a generation ago. The rate of change is increasing at a phenomenal rate. Whereas once a youth would confidently know his or her career as it was the trade or business of the father, now we are told that most of the careers our children will enjoy don't exist yet.

Hewlett Packard, the electronics manufacturer, made most of their profits this year from a product that didn't exist a year ago. How do we cope in such speedy and complex times? And more than cope, how do we thrive?

Margaret Wheatley is an internationally known researcher and author. Wheatley has spent her life studying the nature of human interactions and the impact they have. Wheatley contributed the list below of the five conversations she feels we must have with our self and others for the sake of our future:

1. **Who is my neighbor?** *Do we know who lives nearby? What do we need to do to get to know each other better?*

    Community is the greatest untapped wealth we have available to us at this time.

2. **How can I cultivate curiosity rather than judgment?**

    It's not our differences that divide us. It is our judgments about our differences. *Are we willing to be curious and listen to the stories of those we've distanced ourselves from?*

3. **What is my role in creating change?** *Am I willing to assume the responsibility for creating the changes I want to see in the world?*

We can no longer wait for leaders or laws to create the changes we need. It's up to us and it's the only way the world ever changes is when a few friends start talking.

4. *Am I willing to reclaim time to think?*

   As the world speeds up we're forfeiting our most precious human capacities -- reflection, awareness, dreaming and relationships. The only way to restore these capabilities is to slow things down, re-engage in reflection, pause and truly notice what's going on.

5. *Can I be fearless?*

   Fearlessness is not being free of fear. It means that we do not allow our fears to silence or stop us. *What issues and people summon me to be fearless?*

It's time to turn off the television, power down the computer, unplug the iPod, and reflect on the potential that each of these conversations hold for our self, our family, our community and our world.

Look for opportunities today to initiate and explore these conversations with those around you. Let us direct the change thoughtfully and respectfully rather than merely react to the change as if we have no power or imagination.

Whenever we exaggerate or demonize, oversimplify or overstate our case, we lose.

~ Barack Obama

The Need for Maturity and Humility

I have just completed reading Barack Obama's book - **The Audacity of Hope - Thoughts On Reclaiming The American Dream** (2008). What Mr. Obama offers is a willingness to dialogue, to consider ideas and perspectives, even those that are different than his own. I was especially moved by the words Mr. Obama spoke in his address following his election as President on November 4, 2008. He stated, *"I will listen to you, especially when we disagree."*

Mr. Obama is of the perspective that our current political discourse is done in such a way as to unnecessarily divide us. He suggests that we are cramped by *"false choices"* when issues are reduced to either-or, for-or-against options. Mr. Bush was the master of polarized choice making when he declared in the days leading up to the invasion of Iraq, *"You are either for us or against us."*

Mr. Obama has the maturity and the humility to recognize that one side does not hold all the wisdom and that holding a majority following an election does not give one the absolute authority to impose their will in the name of the majority.

Our system of economics, governance and community, even our health care is based upon trust. And when the trust is eroded by arrogance, false choices, deceit and dishonesty and polarized thinking our civilization cannot survive.

It is through the process of considered and respectful dialogue, innovative problem solving, and a commitment to shared success that our future safety and stability is secured.

I believe people are ready for a maturing of discourse whereby ideas and strategies can be genuinely debated, their advantages and disadvantages acknowledged, weighed, and responsibly considered.

Then the hard choices that need to be made are made, not based upon party lines, not based upon winning and losing, not based on the results of the latest polls, not based on the most economic gain, but rather based upon what is the *best option possible* to address our current challenges. Obama states that our politics is more committed to *"winning than to solving problems"* and as such fails to utilize all of the wisdom within a community.

The need for a maturing of our political process is not solely the responsibility of our politicians. Citizens too need to move beyond their polarized silos. We need to refuse to engage in divisive either-or thinking. We need to become better informed on the merits and risks of each possibility and be willing to debate our neighbors, our elected officials, and our authorities with honesty and integrity.

We need to view compromise and collaboration, not as weakness, but as strength. We need to monitor our progress and have the courage to admit that a chosen course of action may not be working. We may need the freedom that humility offers to choose again.

It is only through maturity and humility that we will advance as a society.

Manufacturing Consensus

The world is a complex and complicated place. It is impossible for each of us to understand and evaluate all that is presented to us on a daily basis. In our efforts to manage the complexities of life we take short cuts. We trust. We trust in the wisdom and integrity of others to inform us on matters that we are unable to research and evaluate for ourselves.

Where the trust is earned and has integrity the trust can serve us well. It releases us of the burden of figuring everything out for our self and allows us to focus our attention and energy in specific areas of interest and passion. Unfortunately our trust in institutions, organizations and authority is being eroded because honesty and integrity is being sacrificed in the interest of profit and power.

At one time we could rely on the declaration that consensus was reached. Consensus is a powerful tool that is regularly used to reassures us that a particular perspective or course of action has been well researched, discussed, debated, and a conclusion reached based on solid evidence. Efforts are made to reassure us by the power of consensus whether the issue is the safety of genetically modified organisms (GMOs), the validity of climate change, the safety and effectiveness of vaccinations, the quality and integrity of industrial safeguards, or even the need for war.

Unfortunately, according to Jon Rappoport, author of **The Matrix**, the process of consensus building has become much less collaborative and evidence based and is more often "*manufactured*".

The *manufacture of consensus* looks like the following:

1. An 'authority', often unnamed, declares an idea or a perspective as fact.

2. Respected individuals, groups, governmental organizations, and the media repeat the authoritative message over and over as if it is fact.

3. The position is taken that because consensus has been reached further discussion and debate is no longer needed or tolerated.

4. Critics and dissenters of the consensus position are attacked. Shock and dismay is expressed that there are *"still people who refuse to accept the obvious"*.

5. Warnings are issued and dire consequences predicted if everyone does not accept the consensus idea or perspective.

6. Carefully constructed "scientific" studies are produced to support the consensus position.

7. A declaration is made that the consensus idea or position represents *'the greatest good for the greatest number'*.

8. Legalized coercion through the introduction of new laws and regulations is introduced to prevent anyone from holding or expressing a dissonant opinion or position.

9. Any dissenter is relegated to the margins and dismissed with labels that deny them a voice or any credibility regardless of their experience or stature.

10. Eventually no one can recall a time when the original idea was seriously disputed.

Science once offered us confidence that a statement, fact, or conclusion was true based upon a rigorous and verifiable process using the scientific method. This is an accepted method to produce verifiable data that will serve in the best interests of truth. Unfortunately the scientific method, a process of hypothesis, data collection, analysis, and confirmation or refusal of the hypothesis has been corrupted.

Where once we could trust the scientific method, today science is begin co-opted for economic and political gains and no longer is a valid seal of approval. Science, like other aspects of our society, has been corrupted by power and politics and is no longer in service to the truth. It is in service to those in power and who have enough money to determine the outcome of science. Consider the two quotes below from editors of science/medical journals:

"It is simply no longer possible to believe much of the clinical research that is published or to rely on the judgment of trusted physicians or authoritative medical guidelines.
I take no pleasure in this conclusion, which I reached slowly and reluctantly over my two decades as an editor of the __New England Journal of Medicine__."

~ Dr. Marcia Angell

"The case against science is straightforward: much of the scientific literature, perhaps half may simply be untrue.
Science has taken a turn toward darkness."

~ Richard Horton, Editor in Chief, __Lancet__

Rappoport explains that these efforts to manufacture consensus are effective because people have a minimal tolerance for conflicting views on a subject of key importance. He believes humans are wired for consensus and prefers consensus to difference.

While consensus is certainly desirable, the question is whether the consensus is based on solid, supported evidence and whether the good that is being promoted is indeed for the greater good, or whether the consensus has been *manufactured* and is actually in the good of a small group of individuals or organizations?

We need to be more discerning of whether the consensus is worthy of our respect.

> *Who is the individual or group declaring there is consensus?*
> *Is there integrity in their decision-making process?*
> *Is there a willingness to allow the science to speak for itself or is there investment in a particular outcome?*
> *Are there economic, political or strategic interests that can compromise the integrity of the decision?*
> *Is there independent access to the information and supporting data?*
> *Are we taking too many short cuts and giving away our responsibility for discernment to those who have not earned our trust?*
> *Are we unduly influenced by the authority of government, the medical community, and the media?*
> *Are we willing to think for ourselves?*

We would be wise to be cautious in accepting consensus positions when other motives are involved that can corrupt a true consensus process.

*Let's be clear: the work of science has nothing whatever
to do with consensus. Consensus is the business of politics.*

*There is no such thing as consensus science.
If it's consensus, it isn't science.
If it's science, it isn't consensus. Period.*

*I regard consensus science as
an extremely pernicious development
that ought to be stopped cold in its tracks.*

*Historically, the claim of consensus
has been the first refuge of scoundrels;
it is a way to avoid debate
by claiming that the matter is already settled.*

~ Michael Crichton, M.D.

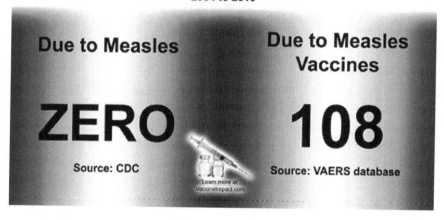

Deaths in the U.S. during the past 10 years:
2004 to 2015

Due to Measles

Due to Measles
Vaccines

ZERO

108

Source: CDC

Source: VAERS database

http://vaccineimpact.com/2015/zero-u-s-measles-deaths-in-10-years-but-over-100-measles-vaccine-deaths-reported

Manufacturing A Crisis

Recently a medical crisis was declared. The result was a tremendous outpouring of anger, resentment and judgment. People were called names. Consideration was given to removing a parent's right to make medical decisions with regards to their children. Some even advocated for removing the children from those parents who didn't comply with the proclaimed action needed to ward off the impending medical crisis.

The crisis that triggered this outpouring of anger and judgment - an outbreak of measles. The media has been incredibly vigilant in reporting the few hundred cases of measles diagnosed in recent weeks. By last count there have been 375 cases reported in British Columbia, six in Calgary, one in Edmonton, eleven in Regina and eleven in Ontario (**Huffington Post**, April 13, 2014).

Individuals of my age are a bit mystified by the intensity of the purported crisis. As someone who grew up in the 1960s everyone I knew contracted measles at some point in his or her childhood. Up until twenty-five years ago almost 100% of children contracted measles. But suddenly a measles outbreak is resulting in a reaction as intense as the SARS crisis of a few years ago, or the AIDS epidemic even prior.

How did this common event become so disconcerting that normally kind and well-intended individuals feel compelled to treat others badly?

Two colleagues shared with me the impact of this purported crisis on their lives. One, the mother of a four year old, informed me that she finally succumbed to having her daughter vaccinated for measles after a barrage of phone calls day after day insisting that she *"do the right thing and get her daughter vaccinated"*. *"You won't be able to live with yourself if your daughter gets measles"* she was informed.

The second, another mother, shared with me the following:

"Hey, there's a measles outbreak! Have you heard? It's got just a wee bit of media attention. I'm having a difficult time filtering out the unkind things people have to say about people who do not vaccinate. Selfish. Should be kept in a bubble/sent to an island/excluded from society. Stupid. Negligent. It's amazing how nasty people can be and how it is apparently okay to suddenly become unkind about parental choices when the topic is vaccination."

I've received my own dose of unkind words and judgments when I've attempted to defend the rights of parents to make an informed decision with regards to vaccinations. **CTV News** reporter Jon Woodward holds people like me responsible for the reduction in vaccination rates in his commentary - **'BC Vaccination Rates Drop Amid 'Misinformation' campaign**. Mr. Woodward is typical of most media pundits in his assessment that I am *"misinformed"*. His failure to provide or demand any evidence of vaccine safety and effectiveness is not considered relevant.

The **National Post** conducted a survey to elicit opinions on whether vaccinations ought to be mandatory and thus denying a parent the right and responsibility to choose what is in the best interests of their child. Not surprisingly, given the bias in the media's reporting of this complex topic, most Canadians support denying a parent the right to make this decision.

This event is similar to numerous other events over the years. Witness the reporting on 9/11 and the invasions of Iraq and Afghanistan. We were inundated with information that was purported to be true by well meaning experts. Remember those weapons of mass destruction? Some kind of urgent action is needed we were told. There is no time to think. There is no time to discuss the matter. Anyone who does not respond as demanded is somehow irresponsible, selfish or delusional.

Author and speaker David Icke has made considerable effort over the years to explain how it is that we are so easily seduced into a reactive response. He describes the process as *'Problem - Reaction – Solution'*. A *problem* is manufactured. A *reaction* is elicited. And a *solution* is offered. Witness the recent events: *measles outbreak = crisis = this is terrible and something must be done = take away a parent's right to choose the medical treatments for their healthy child.*

We would be wise to be more discerning in how we are coerced into making reactive decisions rather than thoughtful and well-informed decisions. We ought to be especially sensitive to situations where we become emotionally hijacked and insist on an immediate solution without the benefit of thoughtful discourse.

These reactive actions undermine our capacity to use our gifts of intelligence and compassion. We all deserve better. The answer will not be to change the way media reports these issues. Rather the answer will be our unwillingness to become easily coerced and distracted from the real issues at hand.

"All truth passes through three stages.
First, it is ridiculed.
Second, it is violently opposed.
Third, it is accepted as being self-evident."

~ Arthur Schopenhauer,
German philosopher (1788 – 1860)

Vaccinations: Science or Religion?

We pride ourselves on being smarter, more conscious and more evolved than the humans beings that came before us. We find it deplorable that previous generations believed in bloodletting, witches, exorcisms, slavery, forced sterilization, religious dogma, literal interpretation of the bible, criminalization of homosexuals, the divine right of Kings and Queens, etc.

Have we fully evolved? Are there no other areas of blindness, dogma, false belief, or unsubstantiated claims of what everyone 'knows to be true'? What might we accept today as truth, fact, and undeniable that a future generation would scoff at, find incredulous, and dismiss as the thinking of a primitive species?

One practice I propose future generations will undoubtedly question is our current medical practice of injecting a mixture of viruses, chemical preservatives, animal products, heavy metals and toxins into the human body, especially our infants. We refer to this practice as vaccination.

Many readers will scoff at this statement and treat any expression of concern about the safety and effectiveness of vaccinations as the ranting of a lunatic, Luddite, anti-science fool who ought to be immediately silenced and dismissed. Such is the power of the belief in the *"miracle of vaccinations"*.

The belief in vaccinations is so strong that even discussion of the issue is denied. Mainstream media has embraced the practice of suppressing any debate on the safety and effectiveness of vaccines.

So convinced are we on the merit of vaccines that a censorship exists to prevent giving voice to those who might entertain such false beliefs.

"There is consensus in the medical community" we are told. *"All vaccines are safe and effective"*. End of story. No further discussion or investigation is needed. Allowing discussion or debate would give credibility where no credibility is due. This would be *'false balance'*.

The typical messages that are routinely delivered in mainstream media and presented as 'facts' whenever questions of vaccine safety are raised –

> *"Vaccines are safe and effective."*
> *"Vaccine injury is one in a million."*
> *"The benefits of vaccination far outweigh the risks."*
> *"We have a social responsibility to vaccinate."*
> *"The science on vaccines is clear."*
> *"Vaccines do not cause autism."*

Unfortunately none of these statements are scientific facts. These statements are opinions and promotional statements. They are **propaganda masquerading as science**.

Saying all vaccines are safe and effective is like saying all prescription drugs are safe and effective. The statement also implies that *all* vaccines are safe and effective for *all* people, which obviously isn't true. The **US Vaccine Court** has awarded more than three billion dollars in compensation for vaccine injury since 1986.

Anyone who states: *"the science regarding vaccinations is clear"* is either not a scientist or is not being honest.

The undisputed facts are the following:

- There are no long-term clinical trials that demonstrate vaccine safety.

- Most effectiveness trials are limited to the measurement of anti-bodies/titers in the blood, rather than producing verifiable evidence that the vaccine actually prevented the targeted disease.

- No safety trials exist that determine the safety of giving multiple vaccinations at once.

- No large safety trials exist that use an unvaccinated population as the control group.

- The current vaccine schedule has never been tested for safety in the real world way in which the schedule is implemented.

- No clinical proof exists to support the claim that vaccines are primarily responsible for the decline in infectious diseases, let alone the claim of millions of lives saved.

- There is <u>no</u> independent biological science that shows injecting mercury into humans is safe in any amount.

- The amount of aluminum used in vaccines regularly exceeds the maximum amount permitted by the FDA.

Unfortunately facts are not part of the discussion when it comes to vaccinations because there is no discussion.

Vaccinations are the new religion. Doctors and the pharmaceutical industry are the new high priests. It is blasphemy to question the edicts of the high priests. The punishment for questioning the edicts of the high priests is being silenced, ostracized, and banished.

Everyone must believe. Anyone who does not believe is a threat to the community. Fear of damnation is used to coerce compliance with the prevailing dogma. Laws must be put in place to secure the compliance of those who do not believe. Witness the mandating of vaccines in California recently. Parents there no longer get to decide what is injected into their children.

The strength of this dogma will be evident in the emotional response to this essay. Many will immediately dismiss what has been presented here. The dismissal will not be based on verifiable scientific evidence. It will not be based on well-designed and critically evaluated clinical evidence of safety and effectiveness. Rather the dismissal will be based on a *belief* of what everyone knows to be true. No evidence is required to demonstrate what everyone already knows to be true.

Then in some future time, when a shift in consciousness occurs, the thought of injecting toxins into babies will be viewed as highly irresponsible and relegated to the mysteries of a primitive species along side bloodletting, belief in a flat earth, and the superiority of one race over another.

The challenge of being asleep is that you don't know you are asleep until you wake up.

Remembering the Consequences of War

As I sat in the sunshine enjoying a hot cup of coffee at a local coffee shop I happened to overhear two mothers discussing a rather timely topic. Her son, declared one of the women, had just enrolled in the Army reserves. While wanting to support her son's initiative, she also shared her deep desire that he not enlist with the military. *"I probably sound like a bad mom in saying that."* she reflected.

The other mother nodded. *"No, I understand. My brother joined the Navy when he was 18. My mother wasn't very pleased about his decision but there wasn't much she could do."* she lamented. *"It didn't turn out very good for him. He became an alcoholic and drug addict and was never the same person again."*

What is it that attracts our young men and women to war? Is it the opportunity for glory? Is it the perception or hope that somehow they can do some good in the world?

I personally have never understood the attraction to the military. I can't even bring myself to wear a poppy on Remembrance Day. Wearing a poppy seems to make me complicit in an organization whose efforts are delivered via rifles, bombs and other means that ensures the destruction of whatever is the focus of its target.

As a society we seem to have a short memory when it comes to remembering the consequences of war. Or maybe the military with the support of the government and media have effectively convinced us that war is necessary, even honorable.

I remember the pronouncements in the dark days following September 11th, 2001. There was no question that a war would be waged. It wasn't a question of *if* but *when*? The voices that attempted to consider an alternative response were quickly drown out. *Naïve. Unpatriotic. Supporting the enemy,* were the refrains.

Sometimes I wonder what a more advanced species would think were they able to look in on the present human condition. Would they understand such behaviors or would they close their eyes and weep?

I'm told the loudest cheers for Mr. Harper at the recent Conservative Party convention in Calgary was in response to Harper's stated intention to increase military spending.

What do these people see that I don't see? What do they know that I don't know? What do they value that I don't value?

I'm honestly perplexed by any human being who would choose to increase military spending rather than increase health care, improve the environment, or raise the level of support for our most vulnerable citizens.

I long for the wisdom of someone of the stature of Henry David Thoreau. Thoreau was best known for an essay entitled **Civil Disobedience** (1942). The essay was Thoreau's response to his 1846 imprisonment for refusing to pay a poll tax that violated his conscience.

When his friend Ralph Waldo Emerson visited Thoreau in jail and asked, *"Henry, what are you doing in there?"* Thoreau replied, *"Waldo, the question is what are you doing out there?"* Following his release Thoreau returned to Walden to mull over the question: *Why do some men obey laws without asking if the laws are just or unjust?*

I long for the day when this human condition has transcended the need for war. For that to happen the investment in peace and peacemaking must be substantially greater than it is today. In the meantime I commit myself to being a peaceful human being and raising the possibility that peace is possible without going to war first.

9/11: Defining Our Consciousness

Another anniversary of the event known as 9/11 has come and gone. In addition to the various events to honor the dead there was significant commentary on the impact of 9/11 and how this event defines and determines our relationship with one another, our governments and our Nation-to-Nation relationships. All of us have been impacted by the events of 9/11 in one way or another.

Of all the articles and commentaries I read on the topic of 9/11 the most powerful and provocative was the commentary provided by Julius Sequerra entitled, **9/11: The Defining Line of Conscience** (The Agora, September 2013). Sequerra presents 9/11 as *the* defining event of our generation and possibly our lives. He states, *"It would be safe to say everyone in every field of endeavor the world over can be defined by their position on this one seminal event."*

By now the vast majority of world citizens realize that the entire events of 9/11 was a charade; a carefully scripted and choreographed event to manipulate the human consciousness into accepting and supporting ongoing military action that continues to this day.

As a result of this diabolical act of deception major wars have been launched, over a million people have died and another five million people displaced. A number of middle Eastern countries are occupied by foreign militaries, natural resources and assets confiscated, privacy and rights violated and there is no end in sight to this treachery.

Sequerra goes on to state - "*And every one of these violations is based on a lie.*" His question to the reader is - "*Do you have the consciousness to acknowledge the lie? Do you have the courage to challenge the lie? Or do you become complicate by maintaining the lie?*" He declares that everyone everywhere can be measured according to this litmus test.

Sequerra invites each of us to –

> "*Think about what you allow yourself to know. Think about what you pass by, ignore, deny, and defend. That defines you. It defines the degree of your personal courage, your relationship with truth, your values, your principles and what you will pass on to your children and everyone you meet.*"

What does the litmus test of 9/11 say about you? What does it say about our leaders, media, governments, organized religions, law enforcement and our justice system? "*It tells you, in that place where your conscience lives (or once lived), whether you are a hypocrite and a fool or whether something greater still lives within you.*" says Sequerra.

I understand people's fear and unwillingness to speak the truth about 9/11. People in government who questioned the official 9/11 story have been fired from their jobs or driven from office by members of their own party. University professors have been dismissed for discussing the topic in their classrooms. Independent experts, investigators and journalists who became too troublesome met with sudden and unforeseen circumstances including death. The intimidation is real and dangerous. Doing the right thing is not easy.

Like Sequerra I believe the time of choosing is approaching. Life has become a giant litmus test.

What will your litmus test reveal?

What is your relationship with truth?

What are you choosing by your words and actions today?

What are your values and principles?

The small band of courageous souls who risk everything to tell the truth - Edward Snowden, Bradley Manning, David Icke, and Julian Assange, encourages me. May they be the leading edge of a tsunami of truth that will dispel and displace the lies and deception that dominates our collective consciousness.

But ultimately this is an individual battle; an individual test.

Do you have the courage to confront power with truth? Or will you stay safe in the manipulated and scripted illusion of what happened on 9/11?

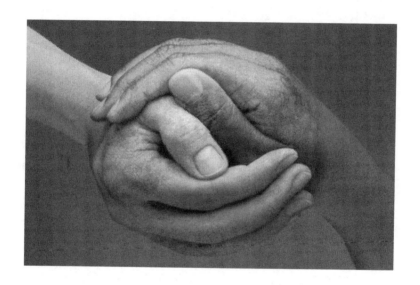

Global Vision

Someone asked me today, *"How do you maintain your peace in the face of so much struggle and adversity?"* Their inquiry was with regards to my profession as a Psychotherapist. The assumption is that I'm exposed to a deluge of negative stories day after day.

The truth is that I'm not exposed to a deluge of negative stories in my professional work. I have the luxury of working with people who recognize they have a challenge and are committed to finding a solution. The work is humbling, inspiring and gratifying.

My ability to maintain my peace and my joy is more deeply challenged by the collective state of our world, especially at a national and international level. Though I work hard to limit my exposure to drama and negativity it is difficult to keep myself insulated, especially when every newscast and newspaper speaks of the possibility of another war being initiated.

I'm disheartened to observe President Obama, whom I had great hope for, leading the argument for another war. I can be moved to despair when I witness the insanity of using military action as a way to address global conflict. To suggest that bombs and other weapons of mass destruction be used to *"punish"* a Nation strikes me as the thinking of a very primitive species.

However, I've discovered that where I place my *'attention'*, and what I set as my *'intention'* determines my experience.

After wallowing in my despair at the thought of more global destruction I received an email from a colleague inviting me to join in creating a spiritual community. The email read:

> *Like me, if you've been looking for a place to explore, grow and connect in spiritual awareness with amazing people, I would LOVE to have you join me is a special gathering. Your input and presence are treasured!*

> *During this special gathering we will be sharing in music, spiritual practice and rich conversation about what we want to explore within ourselves, what moves our hearts, and what we desire to create, share and embody in our spiritual growth as we evolve--together.*

Upon further exploration I discovered that this spiritual community holds the following global vision:

- *We envision all people, all beings, and all life as expressions of God.*

- *We see a world in which each person lives in alignment with his/her highest spiritual principle, emphasizing unity with God and connection with each other; a world in which individually and collectively we are called to a higher state of consciousness and action.*

- *We envision humanity awakening to its God-Given spiritual magnificence and discovering the creative power of thought; a world where each person discovers his/her own personal power and ability to create an individual life that works within a world that works for everyone.*

- *We envision a world in which we live and grow as One Global Family that respects and honors the interconnectedness of all life; a world where this kinship with all life prospers and connects through the guidance of spiritual wisdom and experience.*

- *We envision a world where personal responsibility joins with social conscience in every area of the political, corporate, academic and social sectors, providing sustainable, structures to further the emerging global consciousness.*

- *We envision a world where each and every person has enough food, a home and a sense of belonging; a world of peace and harmony, enfranchisement and justice.*

- *We envision a world in which resources are valued, cared for, grown and there is generous and continuous sharing of these resources.*

- *We envision a world-wide culture in which forgiveness, whether for errors, injustices, or a debt is the norm.*

- *We envision a world that has renewed its emphasis on beauty, nature and love through the resurgence of creativity, art and aesthetics.*

- *We envision a world that works for everyone and all of creation.*

After reading this global vision my heart filled with hope and inspiration and I affirm that if there is to be a better world, then it is up to me to create it.

And so I dust myself off, hold my vision, and find like-minded souls to work with.

*We're looking for women with roots in this community
who want to give back and support young women
to perhaps take different paths than they did.*

~ Janice Abbott, Executive Director
Atira Women's Resource Society

Little Sister

Atira Women's Resource Society (www.atira.bc.ca) is breaking new ground. Literally. Last week marked the opening of a 'first in Canada' housing project. A 12-unit housing development has been constructed in Vancouver's downtown east side using recycled shipping containers.

On a piece of property that would normally accommodate one detached home, the Atira Women's Resource Society is able to provide housing for twelve individuals. The economic savings of this innovation reduces the costs of home construction from approximately $200,000.00 per unit to $80,000.00 per unit.

The best part of this housing innovation however is not the shipping containers. It's the mix of people that will occupy these homes. Six of the twelve residences are reserved for women over the age of 50. The reason for this is suggested by the name of the housing project – *'Imouto'*.

Imouto is a Japanese word that means *"little sister"*. The richest innovation of this project is the intention to connect older women with younger women in an intergenerational mentoring. Janice Abbott, Executive Director of Atira, describes their selection criteria in this way - *"We're looking for women with roots in this community who want to give back and support young women to perhaps take different paths than they did."*

While the logical part of me is thrilled with the innovative use of shipping containers, the heart in me is moved by their vision to build networks of support for vulnerable women. As the father of a son with disabilities I carry constant worry over whether my son is safe. My journey in the disability community has taught me an importance lesson - *relationships are the key to safety.*

Research has demonstrated that our safety is dependent upon the number of relationships we have. The more relationships, the safer we are. The fewer relationships, the more vulnerable we are. Unfortunately, we often fail to recognize how essential relationships are to creating a good life.

We are more likely to rely on the technological resources available to us rather then nurture the relational resources that surround us. We are more likely to invest in sophisticated locking and alarm systems then to invest in developing the informal system of connection between neighbors.

A number of years ago **The Search Institute** in the United States examined the qualities of successful children.

Their research identified forty components of success. They labeled these components 'assets'.

One of the more interesting assets they uncovered is that a child's success is dependent upon the number of neighbors who know the child by his or her first name.

In our efforts to keep our children safe we travel in exactly the opposite direction and employ the opposite strategy. We advise our children – "Don't talk to strangers".

The fact is only one to two percent of the population is a risk to our children, and ninety-eight to ninety-nine percent are a potential source of support. In our efforts to protect our children from the one or two percent we fail to build relationships with the greater part of a community that can help our children succeed.

Wouldn't it be wonderful if everyone under the age of fifty had a 'big sister' or "big brother' to guide them, and everyone over the age of fifty had a 'little sister' or "little brother' to be the recipient of their love and wisdom?

If we want to create a kinder and safer world we need to build relationships.

Unless someone like you cares a whole awful lot.
Nothing is going to get better.
It's not.

~ The Lorax – Dr.Suess

Any Change Is Up To Us

A few weeks ago I watched the documentary, **The Fix**. It was one of the offerings at the Vancouver Oceans Film Festival.

The Fix chronicles the efforts made by British Petroleum (BP) to fix the damage created in the Gulf of Mexico following an explosion on their deep water drilling rig a couple of years ago. The documentary wasn't about BP's efforts to stop the gushing of oil into the Gulf. Rather it was about BP's efforts to "*fix*" the public's perception of the problem; to cover-up the massive damage being done to marine and human life in the areas affected by the toxic spill.

The documentary left me feeling deep sadness about our human condition. The profound disregard and ongoing damage to the environment and to fellow human beings eroded my confidence in the goodness of this modern civilization. What became clear from the documentary is that industry and governments are NOT acting in the best interest of citizens but rather are colluding in the best interest of shareholders, politicians and executives who wish to remain in power.

What was most disconcerting however was not the decision made by the top-level executives of British Petroleum to cover up the spill. Rather it was that many hundreds of individuals implemented the destructive and dishonest plans of BP.

It's easy to blame BP's Chairman and CEO and believe that these individuals are greedy and irresponsible. And while this is undoubtedly true the truth is even more disturbing.

The damage and the deception that continues to impact the marine and human life in the Gulf of Mexico is not made by these executive's own individual efforts. The CEO and Chair of BP have no more power to wreak havoc on the environment or deceive the American people than G.W. Bush did to start the wars in Iraq and Afghanistan.

The cover-up currently taking place on the beaches of Louisiana is being done by hundreds of machine operators, boat operators, airline pilots, security guards and laborers who collectively are covering up any evidence of oil on the beaches and the decaying of marine life on the shores.

A couple of months ago I was chastised by a reader who took offense to my newsletter entitled **Root Causes** where I invited readers to recognize that we are all at root cause to the damage and destruction that we see each day on our televisions. The reader was incensed with my comments and demanded I remove her name from my mailing list. I wish the solution were that easy.

In a recent Vancouver Courier column (**Multinationals Stick to Their Guns**, June 7, 2013), columnist Geoff Olson chronicled the dependence our largest multinationals have on the waging of war. Companies as Volvo, Caterpillar, John Deere, Samsung, Panasonic, Dell, Hyundai, Mitsubushi, and Rolls Royce are all making huge profits building weapons of mass destruction.

But these weapons are not made by them self. Many thousands, possibly hundreds of thousands of individuals strap on their boots everyday or take briefcases in hand and show up for work to design, build, transport, maintain and advertise these weapons.

I appreciate that this kind of change in direction takes courage and sacrifice. Witness the courage and sacrifice of Edward Snowden, the former National Security Agency contractor who blew the whistle on the widespread invasion of privacy by the US Government. Mr. Snowden is currently "*in transit*" in Moscow in an effort to avoid being incarcerated for the rest of his life by the US Government for speaking the truth.

Witness the sacrifices made by WikiLeaks publisher Julian Assange, and USA Army Private Bradley Manning whose lives are in a state of peril as a result of disclosing US documents that provide evidence of massive wrongdoing by the US Government.

Yet, if we are to make a change in our direction, if we are to live respectfully and sustainably on this planet, if we are to value peace above war, we need more people to act courageously like Snowden, Assange and Manning.

They are my new heroes.

Enlightened Self Interest

The following story comes from author Victor Chan. The setting for this story is the Indian city of Bodhgaya. Located within Bodhgaya is the sacred Mahabodhi Temple, the site where the Buddha is considered to have attained his enlightenment twenty-five hundred years ago. The Dalai Lama regularly participates in a ritual at the temple to honour and acknowledge the wisdom and teachings of the Buddha.

During one such occasion the Dalai Lama, in walking between the temple and the monastery, abruptly changes his direction. He approaches a large group of Tibetans straining to gain the attention of their spiritual leader. In the group is a young man seated on the ground next to an old woman. The young man, in his early twenties, has a cane in one hand. Although the man's eyes are open the Dalai Lama correctly surmises the man is blind.

The Tibetan monk bends down, takes the man's hand in his, and speaks with him. The Dalai Lama wants to know where the man has come from and whether he has received any medical treatment for his blindness.

He learns the young man and his elderly mother are from a distant part of Northeast Tibet. The young man lost his sight at age fifteen after a fall. Over the years his mother has tried desperately to find treatment for her son. Nothing has worked. The man's optical nerves are badly damaged and he has been told he will never see again.

When the young man heard that the Dalai Lama would be in Bodhgaya he was determined to go. Family and friends tried to dissuade him, telling him that the journey would be arduous and dangerous. But the young man was determined. And so his mother sold all of her jewelry and cattle and borrowed from relatives and friends to finance the trip.

While the opportunity to meet and speak with the Dalai Lama was more than the young man could have hoped for, there is more to this story. On his journey to India the young man and his mother stayed in various camps along the way. Often the camps were simple canvas tents where the pilgrims would stop to eat and sleep on their way to Bodhgaya. The blind man was in a tent with eight or ten others. One of the fellow travelers who shared the same tent was a young Tibetan monk from South India.

After only a few days of companionship with the blind man the young monk decides to donate his eyes to the blind man. Eye donation from an individual who has recently died is a relatively common event. The donation of one's eyes by a living person is unheard of. Yet this is the gift the young monk offered the blind man.

The blind man thought long and hard about the monk's offer. He was tremendously moved by the generosity of the monk. In the end he refused the monk's offer. He explained his refusal by saying that he had suffered tremendously over the years because of his blindness and he simply couldn't bear the thought of another person going through the same challenges and agony he had experienced.

From the outside it could be said that nothing happened - the blind man continued his life as a blind man. And yet something beautiful, intangible and immeasurable happened.

A deep expression of compassion was expressed. Hearts were opened. Love was given, received, and returned.

The Dalai Lama explains the power of compassion in this way. He says compassion is more than a sense of caring and concern for others. For the Dalai Lama compassion is the source of health and peace of mind. He explains –

> *"If we think only of ourselves and forget about other people, then our minds occupy a very small area. Inside that small area, even tiny problems appear big. But the moment you develop a sense of concern for others your mind automatically widens. At this point your own problems, even big problems, will not be so significant. The result is an increase in peace of mind."*

The Dalai Lama summarizes his perspective on the importance of compassion by saying –

> *"If you think only of yourself, only of your own happiness, the result is actually less happiness."*

He deeply understands that when we have compassion and are of help to others, we are the first to benefit. He calls this principle *"enlightened self interest"*.

May we all have enlightened self-interest.

How might our actions as individuals, organizations,
corporations and governments
be contributing
to the attitudes of our young people?

Exploring Root Causes

When my son began to convulse following a routine childhood vaccination at five months of age I was surprised by the complete disinterest of our medical system in understanding the root cause of his intense seizing. The Doctor explained, *"We're not really interested in the underlying cause as it doesn't change how we treat the condition."*

I saw the same philosophy expressed last week following the detonation of two bombs at the Boston marathon. In the after wake of the event Justin Trudeau, the newly elected leader of the Liberal Party, expressed interest in understanding the root causes of the actions taken by the then unknown suspects.

Not unlike the medical example cited above, Prime Minister Harper and his cohorts dismissed Mr. Trudeau's invitation to deepen our understanding of events and behaviors as this. Conservative House Leader Peter Van Loan described Mr. Trudeau's comments as being *"soft on terrorism"*.

I'm disturbed by the unwillingness of our governments and media to better understand root causes. I wonder if our reluctance might be due to the recognition, however minimal, of our being *complicit* in events and actions as this.

How might our actions as individuals, organizations, corporations and governments be contributing to the attitudes of our young people? Might our disregard for the Earth and continued efforts to poison, destroy and eliminate other species have anything to do with the disenfranchisement of the young?

Might our championing of war, our willingness to spend billions on weapons of mass destruction while large segments of the population are without adequate housing, clean drinking water and access to medical treatments contribute to the anger and hostility expressed by some people?

Might our use of negative campaign ads and the disrespect and even dishonesty routinely expressed by politicians in their effort to win power at all costs contribute to our dismay and disappointment?

Might the fact that banks and large corporations were deemed too big to fail and received billions in bailouts while people with low paying jobs were pushed out of their homes contribute to anger and resentment?

Mr. Harper and others would have us believe that the world is black and white and that any exploration of underlying causes is soft and sentimental; that punishment and a rigid stance is the only way.

Similarly, Mr. Bush and his ideologues had us believe that *"You are either for us or against us"* is the way of a civilized society. Yet how is it civilized when the United States has more people in prison on a per capita basis than any Nation on Earth?

I welcome an exploration of root causes. And I especially welcome an exploration that invites each of us to consider **our own role and responsibility** in the world being the way it is.

I'm reading **JFK and the Unspeakable - Why He Died and Why It Matters** by James Douglas (2010). Douglas uncovers the threat Kennedy posed to the military-industrial complex because of his willingness to consider peace with the enemy.

In contrast to the hard line, polarized and rigid Cold War consciousness of the day, Kennedy was willing to dialogue with the Soviet Union in an effort to create a peace together.

Even more threatening to those who would benefit greatly from a prolonged war was Kennedy's invitation during his 1963 address to the American University to – *"examine our own attitudes and narrowly constructed perspectives that contribute to war"*. It speaks volumes that Kennedy's speech at the American University was heralded throughout the world *except* in his own country.

We can continue to do more of the same and assume the wrongdoing that happens is all about someone else. Or we can examine our role in how this world is constructed and take responsibility for both the damage that is being done on a daily basis, and the solutions to a healthier, kinder and more sustainable world.

It's not about the skill of archery.
Rather, it's a reminder of how to live my day.

~ Harlan Lahti, Founder
Finlandia Natural Pharmacy

Fifty Arrows

Harlan begins each day with arrows. Fifty, to be exact. Not a usual practice in our modern society, yet a practice Harlan indulges in each and every day. *"I feel compelled. I can't start my day without first heading into the back yard and firing fifty arrows."* says Harlan.

"It's not about the skill of archery. Rather, it's a reminder of how to live my day" explains Harlan. *"What is required is focus. As I draw the arrow back in my bow, I remind myself to 'focus on the target'. Look at the target. Focus. Release the arrow. Insert the next arrow in my bow. Pull the string back. Focus. Release the arrow."*

"Life is about focus" says Harlan. Harlan should know. Harlan is a very successful business entrepreneur in Vancouver. As the owner and founder of **Finlandia Natural Pharmacy**, a resource committed to helping people improve their health, Harlan knows the importance of staying focused. It makes all the difference between success and failure.

I too have come to understand the importance of focus. Two of the core principles I use to guide my life are *'intention'* and *'attention'*. **Intention** is about knowing what my goal is; knowing my target. **Attention** is about maintaining my focus on my goal. Having *clarity of intention* and being *unwavering in my attention* is critical to my success.

I had an epiphany many years ago. I came to the sudden realization that my life was focused on the wrong goals. My life was focused on making money, having a nice home, driving a nice car, and pursuing a life of comfort.

One day, after a profound experience with my son, I came to the realization that material possessions and comfort weren't enough; these goals weren't what my heart truly yearned for. I came to the realization that even though I had material abundance I wasn't happy. I wasn't joyful. I wasn't peaceful.

It dawned on me that I wasn't happy, joyful or peaceful because I had not set these as my targets. I had never truly focused on peace, joy and happiness as my goals. I had been lead to believe that I would achieve peace, joy and happiness by having material abundance. That day I realized I needed to shift my target.

Rather than write out a *'to do list'*, I began each day with a *'to be list'*. *Who did I want to be today? How did I want to **be** today?* I placed my focus on *being* rather than *doing*.

Each evening I would review my day and examine how successful I had been in achieving my goal. *Where did I give away my joy? How did I release my peace and happiness? What might I do different tomorrow to maintain my peace, joy and happiness?*

What are your goals each day? If you were to begin your day with fifty arrows, what is the target you would point them at?

Adopting A Traitor's Heart

It is pretty evident things need to change. The impact humans are having on this planet, other species, and one another has been incredibly destructive during this last century. Unless we figure out how to live together in peace and harmony our future is bleak. The evidence of destruction is all around us - endless wars, substantial climate change, rapid extinction of species, GMO, chemical and other widespread contamination.

Fortunately there are many dedicated to change. Some attempt change on an individual level, being the best they can be. Others focus their efforts on whole system transformation, creating a paradigm shift equivalent to the civil rights movement. These individuals think nothing short of a transformation in human consciousness will save us.

One of the individuals dedicated to social innovation is consultant and researcher Dr. Frances Westley. Westley is one of the principles in a Canada wide initiative called **Social Innovation Generation**. Westley is a recognized scholar in the areas of social innovation, strategies for sustainable development, strategic change, visionary leadership and inter-organizational collaboration. She is a co-author of **Getting to Maybe** (Random House, 2006). I had the pleasure of hearing Dr. Westley speak in Vancouver. What I heard resonated deeply with me.

There were a number of messages I took away from the event. One is Westley's belief that *systems can heal themselves*; that we have an innate capacity to heal.

She also believes that the disruption created by a crisis is *necessary* to open up opportunities for change. Individuals and systems don't change unless their status quo has been disrupted.

I recognize this truth from my counseling practice. It is rare for a client to inquire about counseling when all is well in their world. It takes a crisis or some level of suffering to create an opening where people are interested in and committed to making change.

One of the most important messages I heard in Westley's presentation is the requirement to let go of an *'us and them'* perspective. She invited her audience to recognize that each of us is part of *"the system"* and together we have created what we experience today. To move forward and create constructive change two actions are necessary - ***forgiveness*** of self and others and the ***willingness*** to forgo blame.

Westley invited us to let go of *blaming* and instead focus on *learning*. She stated - *"learning is more important than justice"*. Thus, rather than focus our attention on *'who is to blame for things being the way they are'*, to focus on *'what can we learn from our past decisions?'*

One of the most interesting ideas I heard was when Westley spoke of the need to have a *"traitor's heart"*. What she means by a traitor's heart is the willingness to let go of the activist orientation where we position our self *against* another and instead join *with* others, even those we deem our enemies. She declared this action necessary if we are to develop solutions based on what she calls a *'whole system perspective'*.

Westley acknowledged how difficult it is to let go of our activist and righteous orientation and admitted that it may feel to some to be a selling out of one's values.

She encouraged us by describing successes that have occurred when there is a joining together in solving complex challenges.

One local example was when **Greenpeace** was able to let go of its activist orientation and enter into dialogue with **MacMillan Bloedel**, a large forestry company. The result was a forestry strategy that included both *development* and *sustainability*.

Westley has learned that *adversarial relationships freeze innovation*. The result is a continuation of the status quo. Unfortunately the human consciousness seems mired in an adversarial, us against them, blamed-based consciousness.

Witness the intense polarization south of the border as Americans engage in selecting their next President. Rather than rich conversations as to how the United States can be a world leader in solving economic, environmental and human crises, instead the focus is on making the other wrong.

I think Westley is onto something. We need to adopt a traitor's heart. We need to let go of blame and shame, and instead admit our own role in the crises we face. We need to invite the wisdom and perspective of all people and be committed to finding solutions that serve everyone.

The good news is I'm confident a crisis is coming to create an opening for transformation. The question is, *will we take advantage of this opportunity when it presents itself or will we let a good crisis go to waste?*

If I am at war with myself,
I can bring little peace
to my fellow man.

~ Unknown

Disturbing The Peace

Each September 21st the world celebrates **International Day of Peace**. On this date the Peace Bell at the United Nations in New York is rung, and speeches are made about the importance of peace. Unfortunately, even as the bells ring out and leaders express wonderful sentiments about their desire for peace, wars continue unabated.

It is a tragedy that we can't create the peace we so desperately desire. While we may have the desire, it appears we lack the wisdom needed to create peace. We are much more proficient at developing the weapons to wage war, and seem too easily convinced that the path to peace is *through* war.

Bruce Sanguin, an ordained Minister serving a congregation in Vancouver, Canada suggests that our pursuit of peace is misguided. He writes, *"What I've come to realize is that I don't actually believe in peace."* (**The Advance of Love**, 2012) Rather provocative words for a Christian Minister! Sanguin is quick to add, *"Obviously, I believe that the absence of armed conflict is desirable."*

Sanguin explains that what we desire is more than simply peace. A peace established and maintained through violence rather than justice is not success. We have witnessed, and continue to witness, peace that is maintained through acts of violence.

The Roman empire of the past, the now dismantled Soviet Union, the actions of dictators as Gaddafi (Libya), Mubarak (Egypt) and al-Assad (Syria), Israel and Palestine, as well efforts by the United States and NATO (Vietnam, Iraq and Afghanistan) are all attempts to impose peace through acts of violence.

Sanguin understands that *"Peacemaking is rarely peaceful"*. He reminds us that Rosa Parks, Martin Luther King Jr., Gandhi, and Augn San Suu Kyi all *disturbed the peace* of their day. Sanguin says there are times when turbulence and disruption are required to bring about change to systems that are frozen and not life giving.

Sanguin believes true peacemakers are not in the service of absolute peace, but rather *the evolution of self, culture, and social systems.* What these individuals listed above wanted was not merely the absence of conflict but the evolution of entrenched systems of racism, authoritarianism and patriarchy. Sanguin contends the peacemaker must carry both a sword for disruption and the skills to create unity.

How does one discern whether one's use of the sword is for the purpose of creating a peace that is just and life giving or a peace maintained through violence? What is common with each of the examples of heroic peacemakers Sanguin lists is the manner in which their swords were used.

Gandhi's actions, while certainly disturbing to the British rulers, were non-violent. Rosa Parks and Martin Luther King's efforts in challenging the racial structures of America were effected without the use of guns or the killing of people in anger or hate. San Suu Kyi led by the power of ideas and dreams of justice in Burma rather than the power of armed conflict.

I appreciate the contribution Sanguin is making to the peace movement. Our task as peace activists is to strive for peace while recognizing that peace by itself is not enough.

There is a time to disrupt the harmony and demand changes to social structures that are not just, dignified or life giving.

It would seem that now is the time for turbulence. Our current economic, political and environmental structures are in need of significant disruption. May our turbulence be guided by wisdom and love.

It is my hope that in my lifetime we will celebrate International Day of Peace by living in a peace sustained by justice.

If today is the day I die,
it is a good day to die.

~ Little Big Man

Facing My Worst Fear

Those of you who know my story are aware of my journey in making peace with my son's medical condition. Josh was damaged by a childhood vaccine at four months of age and developed an uncontrolled seizure disorder. Initially the frequency of Josh's seizing was once every thirty to forty days.

Over the next few years the rate of seizing increased. By age four Josh was seizing twelve to fifteen times per day. More damaging to his health and development was the length of the seizures. Josh's seizures fluctuated between fifteen and twenty-five minute in duration.

On the odd occasion Josh would seize for hours before medical intervention was able to arrest the seizure. And then there was the memorable time when Josh seized for four days.

The doctors had warned his mother and I that a seizure of twenty minutes expends as much energy as required to run a marathon. My four-year old son was running the equivalent of twelve to fifteen marathons each day. The doctors knew Josh's little body couldn't sustain that level of activity. They informed his mother and I of the harsh reality of Josh's condition - each seizure had the potential to end his life.

For years I lived in chronic fear. Each time Josh seized I held my breath and wondered if my son would die in front of my eyes. And at the end of his seizure when Josh would gasp to reclaim his breath I too would gasp to reclaim my breath.

I remember holding my seizing son in my arms during those four long days of seizing. I felt certain Josh couldn't sustain this ordeal. His mother and I spoke about the real possibility that Josh would leave us at any moment. I recall that moment vividly in both my memory and in my heart. It was that moment when I finally accepted the possibility of Josh passing.

I remember using a phrase borrowed from **Little Big Man** (1970), a Hollywood movie with Dustin Hoffman. In the movie Hoffman makes peace with his own potential death and utters the words –

"If today is the day I die, it is a good day to die."

That day I shared these same words with my son.

The good news is Josh didn't make his transition that day or any day since over these past thirty-one years. Even more valuable was the powerful lesson I learned. I learned the consequence of confronting my worst fear.

In facing my fear, in looking my son's death in the eye and making peace with it, I acquired a peace I had not experienced during the previous four years of my journey with Josh.

I've learned that fear only has power over us when we fail to fully confront whatever it is we fear. Fear grabs us and holds us in its trembling grip, and all the while we look away and do whatever we can to distract from the thoughts that fear evokes.

That day in Royal Columbian Hospital I experienced the power and blessing of confronting my worst fear. I watched how its power evaporated in the light of acceptance. I discovered the liberation that occurs when one accepts what they can't control and faces that possibility squarely.

I've learned that fear can be our worst enemy. It can also be our friend. I've discovered that the suffering that fear evokes can and does lead to a deepening of our wisdom if we will only face what we most resist.

That day twenty-seven years ago, when I met fear unflinchingly I was launched onto a new path. A path filled with peace and acceptance.

For this I am truly grateful.

Joshua Kuntz

He's Lucky To Have You

"He's lucky to have you" said the man sitting in the chair at the end of the row. For the last few minutes he'd been watching my son as Josh explored the waiting room of the chiropractor's office.

The man meant well. His words were spoken with kindness and compassion. I understood what he was getting at. It takes only a few moments to see that my son is different. What causes the searching for a label is Josh's stooped posture, his unsteady gait, saliva running constantly off his lower lip, and Josh's use of words - short, simple. *"Who's that?"* *"What she doing?"* It's the language of a two-year-old. The words are odd when paired with the body of a nineteen-year-old with whiskers on his chin.

The man's statement is true. Josh is lucky to have me. I am in love with my son. I enjoy and appreciate who he is and the gifts he offers. Not everyone responds to Josh this way. Not everyone is able to see Josh's gifts. Not everyone can see past the parts of my son that are disabled to enjoy the parts of him that are lovely and endearing.

For a long time I couldn't get past the disabled parts either. I spent years wishing my son would be normal and healthy. I wanted the doctors to do something. Anything! Just fix him. It took me a while to accept my son for who he is.

But the truth is I am the lucky one.

I'm lucky to have Josh. Josh is the most significant teacher in my life.

Josh opened me up to all kinds of experiences I'd heard about but really didn't understand. Josh forced me to deal with aspects of humanity as anger, sadness, forgiveness and acceptance. Also patience, simplicity, love, and respect for differences. I read about these things in self-help books and textbooks. Josh helped me to find these qualities in my own heart.

Bonnie Sherr Klein, author of the book **<u>Slow Dance</u>** (1997) writes, "*Disability allows the possibility for us to be our most human*". I know I am more *human* because of my relationship with my son. I know that my relationship with Josh has made me more sensitive to the plight of people who are marginalized because of their differences. I know that Josh has challenged me to recognize that gifts come in many shapes and sizes and that the gifts of '*being*' are just as valuable as the gifts of '*doing*'.

And so the truth is we are both lucky. We are lucky to have each other. Both of us have grown immensely as a result of this relationship. Josh is a better person because of knowing me, and I am a better person because of knowing Josh.

Josh isn't special in this way. All people have something valuable to offer. All people have the ability to make a contribution. When I meet a person in my day I consciously ask myself, "*What gift does this person have for me?*" "*What gift do I have for them?*" This line of questioning enables me to recognize that each moment, each encounter is precious.

Today a man recognized the gifts I offer my son. Maybe tomorrow he will recognize the gifts my son offers me. And on that day we will celebrate because humanity will be richer for this acknowledgement.

Why Is Everyone Looking At Me?

My friend Sarah recently returned from Spain. Sarah shared with me an interesting experience while there. She described a conversation she had with the owner of the youth hostel where she was staying.

After a few days of touring Barcelona she approached the owner and asked a question. *"Will you be honest with me if I ask you a personal question?"* she inquired. *"I'll try"*, said the owner, *"What's on your mind?"*

"Is my skirt too short?" asked Sarah. *"No, its just fine. It's about the length all the girls are wearing these days."* *"Am I dressed odd in any way?"* asked Sarah. *"No, you look just fine."* replied the owner. *"Then why is everyone looking at me?"* asked Sarah

"Ahhh", said the owner. *"Yes, we do that in Spain. People look at each other. You'll get used to it."*

And Sarah found she did get used to the looks and smiles of others as she went about her day. Sarah discovered she quite enjoyed the sense of connection she shared with absolute strangers.

When Sarah returned home to Canada she was surprised by her experience. She realized Canadian people often don't look at one another as they walk down the street or pass in stores.

"After my experience in Spain I began to enjoy being seen. Now that I'm back home it feels as though I'm invisible. It's as though people look right past me. It feels lonely not to be acknowledged, if only with a nod or a smile, or the confirmation through someone's eyes." declared Sarah.

Maybe Sarah has something here for us to consider. *Do we see one each other as we pass in our day? Do we acknowledge their essence? Do we see beyond the exterior garments and engage, however briefly, the divine essence that blesses us with their presence?*

Are we missing each other? Are we in such a hurry to get to the next place that we miss what is in this place? Are we so focused on completing the next task that we miss out on the beauty of this moment?

Simon, an Australian friend, offers me the same insight. When ever I greet Simon with the standard expression – *"Nice to see you."* Simon's response is always the same. *"It's nice to be seen."*

I like to play a game with myself as I go about my day. As I meet others during the course of a day's activities I silently ask myself the question – *"What gift does this person have for me today?"*

I like to play with the idea that each encounter, no matter how simple or innocuous it may seem is a gift of significant importance.

Have we become so numbed by the busyness of life that we loose the magic of each moment, the miracle of this divine being who engages me and invites me to acknowledge my divinity as I acknowledge theirs?

For years I signed my correspondence with the word 'Namaste'. Namaste is a Sanskrit word that can be translated into the message – "*The Divine in me recognizes the Divine in you."* or *"All that is best and highest in me greets/salutes all that is best and highest in you."*

I'm going to return to that greeting. I'm going to raise my level of consciousness of the gift of the presence of another. I'm going to see in them what they may have forgotten about themselves, and in this way serve to remind all those I meet that they are more than their physical garment, more than their ego identity, more than just this moment in time and space. They are miraculous beings!

And maybe through this reminding we will remember who we all are and what is really important.

Namaste.

You're the one you've been waiting for.

~ Byron Katie, Author
Loving What Is

Has Canada Given Up On Peace?

When asked most Canadians readily declare they value peace. For decades we have prided ourselves on being a peaceful nation and have long held an international reputation as being peacekeepers. Many internationals travelers have been known to sew a Canadian flag onto their backpack as a means to ensure a more welcoming reception in distant lands.

The past however is not the present. Canada no longer presents itself as a peaceful nation committed to peacemaking. If anything the current government prides itself on being a military force to be reckoned with. The recent spending by the Harper Government clears up any misunderstandings that may continue about Canada's role on the international stage.

The Conservative Government of Canada is intent on expanding Canada's military presence both nationally and internationally. Not only has this government committed almost half a trillion dollars to the purchase of F35 fighter jets and the construction of warships and armored vehicles, plans are underway to establish Canadian military bases in countries as Jamaica, Kuwait, and Germany.

Our military presence isn't only evident in the House of Commons and the manufacturing factories producing this military hardware. Average citizens are now exposed to military displays and recruitment drives at summer exhibitions and sporting events. Witness the 2007 Grey Cup trophy entering Toronto's stadium in an armored tank. Even in our citizenship ceremonies a military speaker promotes military service as the highest form of citizenship.

There is an inability amongst our current elected officials to understand that war represents failure - the failure of humanity to address its challenges in more thoughtful and compassionate ways. Instead we are told it is unpatriotic and disrespectful to question the acts of war by one's government and servicemen.

We place more honor on those who die in military battle than those who consciously abstain from the destructiveness of war. The failure of Canada's Immigration Minister, Jason Kenney to grant amnesty to Iraq war resisters living in Canada clearly affirms what values are being embraced.

It is becoming increasingly difficult to view Canada as a civilized country when it prefers to dedicate its resources to fighter planes rather than pensions, warships rather than healthcare, and armored vehicles rather than affordable housing.

If we are truly dedicated to peace what is our commitment to peace? What resources do we dedicate to peace? *Do we have a Department of Peace? Do we have a peace room? Do we have an army of trained individuals dedicated to teaching peace?*

Do we dedicate a sizable portion of our government's financial resources to peace? Do we honor those individuals who refuse to be agents of war and offer them sanctuary in our country?

Costa Rica is one country that does more than talk about peace. This small country has taken significant steps toward the goal of peace. In 1949 Costa Rica abolished its military. It took the financial resources that were dedicated to the military and directed these resources toward education, healthcare and the environment. The result is Costa Rica consistently ranks the highest among the Americas in the **Environmental Performance Index**, the **Happy Planet Index**, and is considered the greenest country in the world.

110

Recently I was in Winnipeg, Manitoba as the guest of David Newman, **Chair of the World Peace Partners**. The Winnipeg Rotarians are determined to make Winnipeg an international centre for peace building and human rights.

Their mission is to advance the concept that each human, regardless where they live or the faith they practice has rights and responsibilities in creating a sustainable and peaceful world. Their goal is to increase awareness that peace begins within oneself and to promote a better understanding of others. They do this by developing and teaching curriculum dedicated to peace, and by building a world-class museum about human rights.

If peace is to be achieved it must begin with each of us making a *commitment* to being peaceful. It must begin with each of us leaning the *skills* and strategies of peaceful decision-making and peaceful conflict resolution. The battlefield that needs to be won does not exist *outside* of us but rather *inside* of us.

Imagination is more important than knowledge.

~ Albert Einstein

Raising Peaceful Children

This week I was invited to speak to parents at a local elementary school. The topic of my presentation was **'Raising Peaceful Children'**. I was delighted at the strong interest shown by parents who were eager to deepen their understanding of how to raise peaceful children. Below is a summary of the information I shared.

I believe raising peaceful children is one of the most important responsibilities we have as parents. Their peacefulness not only benefits the child, it benefits the entire community. When each of us live in peace our peacefulness positively impacts those around us and models a way to live that is inspiring.

Many of us have been raised with the idea that peace happens when things are 'right' in the *outside* world. As a consequence most of our attention is focused on changing outside circumstances or people.

What if peace is an *'inside job'*? What if peace is a *decision* one makes? What if peace is created by the thoughts we hold and the stories we tell ourselves?

My guidance to the parents in attendance that evening was the following:

1. Take 100% Responsibility for Your Thoughts, Emotions, and Actions

Encourage your children to take one hundred percent responsibility for their thoughts, emotions and actions. Assist your children to explore how *they* created their emotions of sadness, hurt and joy. Invite them to be curious about their thoughts and the stories they tell themselves. Challenge your children whenever they use expressions as - *"You make me angry"* or *"You made me do that"*.

2. Use Your Imagination Creatively

Our imagination is a powerful tool. Einstein declared - *"Imagination is more important than knowledge"*. Rather than focusing your attention solely on the *knowledge* your child acquires, ensure that your son or daughter is developing their *imagination*.

Most people use their imagination negatively. They imagine the things they *don't* want to experience. The result is fear and anxiety. Encourage your children to use their imagination positively. Use this incredible tool to imagine what they *want* to create or experience. The result of using their imagination positively is joy and enthusiasm.

3. Take Responsibility For Your Stories.

We are constantly telling our self stories. Most of our stories occur at an unconscious level. Raise the awareness of the stories your children tell them selves as well as the stories they allow to be told to them.

The Native people understood the power of storytelling. They communicated morals, values and life skills to their children through the use of storytelling. Stories engage both the head and the heart. *Who tells the stories your children hear today? Are these storytellers people you know and do they share your values?* Take back the responsibility of storytelling to your children.

4. Live in the Present.

Most of us live in our *mental* body. We spend most of our waking moments in *memory* (the past) or in *anticipation* (the future). Life is best lived in the present moment. When we live in the present life is calmer, richer and more joyful. Encourage your children to get back to their five senses - sounds, sight, taste, touch, and smell. When we intentionally activate one of our five senses we live in our body in this moment.

5. Choose What Does the Most Good.

In each and every moment we have choice. There is no such thing as - *"I have no choice"*. Invite your children to choose what action they will take next. Ask them to consider what action of theirs would *'do the most good'*. Encourage your children to live as *creative* beings rather than *reactive* beings. Creative beings recognize they participate in creating their next experience.

6. Be Happy Now.

Most people think their happiness comes from outside of one self. We use expressions as - *"I'll be happy when . . ."* These kind of expressions delude us into thinking happiness comes from something outside rather than inside.

Happiness, like peace, is an inside job. Abraham Lincoln said - *"Most people are about as happy as they make up their minds to be."*

Invite your children to be happy now with exactly what life has brought them.

7. Breathe From Your Diaphragm.

Our bodies are designed to breathe using our diaphragm. This means that our belly, that part below our naval, ought to rise and fall with each breath. When we breathe from our diaphragm we are grounded and centered - physically, emotionally and psychologically. Regularly remind your children to breathe from their belly, especially during times of upset.

8. Model Peace

The most powerful way to teach peace is through modeling. Children are more influenced by what we *do* rather than what we *say*. When we model peacefulness, especially during times of stress, our children come to understand that peace is a choice we make each and every moment.

Thriving In An Uncertain Future

We are living in uncertain times. The speed of change is increasing rapidly and is not expected to slow anytime soon. Previously change was a temporary period between islands of stability. Today the islands of stability have shrunk and more and more of life is about living in the sea of change.

The skills and attitudes that supported us on solid ground are different than the skills and perspectives required for managing at sea. Below are four ideas to help you thrive in uncertain times.

1. Claim Your Power

Most of us live in a hierarchical structure where those at the top dictate ideas, rules and direction to those lower in the structure. The responsibility for decision-making is located within a small segment of society. This structure might have served us well during the Industrial age when the actions required were relatively simple and straightforward. In today's complex and inter-dependent society we can no longer rely on the wisdom of a few at the top. We all need to be part of the solution.

Nature provides us with a different model of leadership. Research has revealed that a hive of bees, a flock of birds, and a school of fish is fifty times more responsive to its environment than any single bee, bird or fish. If we are to solve today's challenges - financial, environmental and social, we *all* need to take responsibility for identifying and implementing the solutions.

This is not a time to be passive and wait for others to solve our challenges. Our future depends upon each of us claiming our power and our responsibility and being part of the solution.

2. Manage Your Fear

For most, the uncertainty of change scares us. It is not uncommon to move into a place of fear when life becomes unpredictable. The hard reality is that fear will not help us. Fear activates our reptilian brain that essentially has two options - *fight or flight*. Neither of these options is adequate to take us through the level of change required. What is needed is the use of our higher brain where the capacity for *innovation, collaboration, creativity* and *intuition* reside.

The best way to manage our fear is to recognize the core components of fear. Fear is, quite simply, the result of telling a *negative story* about the *future*. I've learned that when I change my story from a negative story to a positive story my emotional body relaxes and allows my higher brain to function.

One story I find helpful during times of change is the story of the caterpillar. There is a time in the life cycle of the caterpillar when it moves into a cocoon and the form and function of the caterpillar dissolves.

From the caterpillar's perspective it is dying. Out of this unformed mass a butterfly emerges with capacity far beyond that of the caterpillar. The story of the transformation of the caterpillar inspires me and reassures me during times of change.

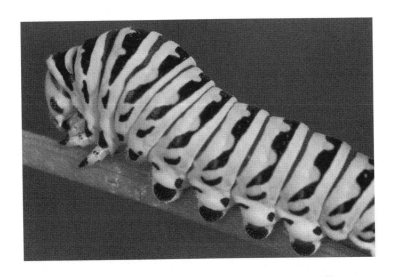

3. Build Your Capacity for Co-Creation

We need to create a culture that invites and honors collaboration and co-creation. Given the need to jointly solve our challenges more focus needs to be given to the power of dialogue and collaboration.

Much of Steve Jobs' success at Apple was due to his commitment to "*deep collaboration*". Jobs insisted that all segments of his company, from engineers to salespeople, be present in the room to generate solutions to their challenges. He referred to this commitment as "*co-engineering*".

We need to 'co-engineer' our next '*way of being*' on this planet. This will require intense dialogue and skilled facilitators who create a culture where everyone feels safe and encouraged to share their ideas and contributions.

I recently visited the Museum of Innovation in Waterloo, Ontario. One of my take-a-ways was the statement:

*"We often imagine the lone scientist in his lab
having a Eureka moment.
The process of innovation is more team-based
and messy."*

4. Work From Your Values

To sustain our self during times of uncertainty it is essential
we understand our values and constantly ground ourselves in
what is important. When confusion strikes we need to remind
ourselves about why we are doing what we are doing. We
also need to allow our values system to evolve over time as
we recognize deeper values and learn new information.

I believe we are all here to make a contribution. In order to
make that contribution we need to have clarity on who we are
and what the bigger picture is. I regularly remind myself of
the story of the church official overseeing the construction of a
cathedral in the Middle Ages.

When the official approached a number of workers and asked
what they were doing each offered a fairly narrow
understanding of their role - building a wall, making a
window, etc. When the official asked an old man who was
sweeping up the shavings left from the day's work, the old
man proudly proclaimed - *"I'm building a cathedral."*

Life is changing and we need to position ourselves to be part
of the solution. *The future literally depends on us.*

Making A Contribution to Humanity

I was inspired by a conversation I had with a colleague today. Milt and I serve on the Board of Directors of **Health Action Network Society** (www.hans.org), a local organization that educates consumers on alternative health treatments. I asked Milt if he was *"winning any battles"*. Milt is a dedicated researcher who is always discovering new and different ideas about the life force that runs through us and around us.

Milt replied, *"We'll see in October."* Milt explained that he and a colleague have been researching the effects of cell phone radiation on the health and well being of humans. He is especially interested in the connection between cell phone use and brain cancer. Milt and his colleague are scheduled to be in U.S. Supreme Court in Washington, D.C. to share the results of thousands of studies on the effects of cell phone radiation on humans.

Milt expressed confidence that he and his partner have accumulated enough evidence to seriously challenge the claims of safety made by the cell phone industry. *"The impact will be huge!"* Milt explained. *"Both in financial compensation to those who have been harmed by cell phone technology, and in changes that will be imposed upon the cell phone industry."*

The potential implications of Milt's research had me concerned for his personal safety. After all, the cell phone industry is a 'Goliath' of an industry.

"Are you concerned about your safety?" I asked. *"I think about it every day"* said Milt. *"How do you cope with that level of risk?"* *"How do you stay committed to your cause when the personal consequences could be high, even life threatening?"*

This is when Milt shared a message that inspires him.

"Antihoch College, a liberal arts college in Yellow Springs, Ohio has a quote placed predominately on their campus." The quote is from Horace Mann's 1859 address at Antioch. *It states:*

"Be ashamed to die
until you have won some victory for humanity".

Milt said this message is what motivates him. This is his mantra. This is what inspires him each day to confront the challenge before him. *"This is my opportunity"* Milt continued, *"to use my knowledge and talents for the betterment of humanity."*

Milt further explained that much of his research is unfunded and he has not received a single pay check in over a year. As a consequence Milt has had to give up his home and move in with friends. *"I have to do this"* said Milt. *"It's important."*

It is individuals like Milt who inspire me. They see life as more than about comfort, acquiring status, wealth or worldly possessions. They are more interested in *giving* than *getting;* in *serving* than in *being served.*

On those days when I'm feeling overwhelmed by the human condition I look to individuals like Milt to remind me that there is much to be grateful for.

Thank you Milt. May you win many battles!

Good Morning God

A couple of weeks ago I was invited to speak to a spiritual congregation in my community. Given it was the beginning of a New Year I wanted to speak about the uncertainty and the potential of the changes before us.

On the morning of the speaking engagement I decided to explore an avenue of reflection I occasionally use. It involves sitting in solitude for a few moments, then with pen and paper, begin a conversation with my Higher Consciousness.

I acquired this method from Neale Donald Walsch, author of **Conversations With God** (1994) Walsch authored many international best sellers in just this way. What follows are the words that emerged when I placed my pen to paper.

Ted: *Good Morning God. I am a bit dismayed and ashamed that I have not sat and connected with you in this way in a very long time. As I read my notes of our conversations from 2001 my heart aches because of the beauty of the messages, and because of my failure to engage you in this way more often.*

Higher Consciousness: *Be gentle with yourself, my son. You and many others, most in fact, do not trust that you can access me this easily. You have been convinced that it must be more difficult than this; that I can only come to you in some other way. But it is just as easy as this.*

I see you are preparing to speak again. Good for you. Thank you for agreeing to do God's work. Thank you for teaching peace. But even more important, thank you for living peace.

Humanity is going through a time of sudden transformation. Be not afraid. It is both an ending and a birthing. Celebrate the birthing and celebrate the endings. Humanity has lived a very long time in ways that are not sustainable. This is about to change. This has to change. I am unwilling to allow you to continue to live in such destructive ways.

Know that I am with you. There will be much change and turbulence. See it all as good. See it as part of the unfolding. Life is meant to be lived joyfully. You have not been living joyfully.

A time has come to change all of that. This is a time of great awakening. Fear not. Yes, there will be endings. Grieve briefly for these endings. Know that what is coming next is even more grand. The human spirit has longed for this day. The time of its birthing has arrived. Celebrate.

What is key at this time of uncertainty and upheaval is to live in peace. Trust in the unfolding. Believe in Divine timing and Divine wisdom. Let go of thinking you know how best for life to unfold.

You will be tested. The answers are simple - **peace, love, joy.** *You can never go wrong if you choose these three paths. Be at peace. This is a grand time. The universe is celebrating your arrival in a higher state of consciousness.*

I Remember

Two years ago I offended the sensibilities of some when I wrote an essay asking the question, *"What are we being asked to remember on Remembrance Day?"* and *"What would be different if we truly remembered?"*

My intent was not to show disrespect or offend anyone. Instead it was my hope to invite further dialogue and consideration about whether we are remembering what we ought to be remembering, and as a result doing all we can to prevent future wars and the loss of human life.

I am not a proponent of military intervention as a means to resolving human conflict. I am of the opinion that the invasions of Afghanistan and Iraq were not only unnecessary, they represent a profound failure of the human condition.

However, rather than invest energy in challenging decisions which have already been made and resisting actions that have already been taken, I prefer to use this Remembrance Day as an opportunity to identify and affirm what I do remember and wish to continue to remember.

I remember:

- Each individual, regardless of color, race, religion, culture or political persuasion is a human being who experiences anger, hurt, fear, love and joy and holds the same aspirations and desires as do the rest of us. There is no 'us' and 'them'. There is only 'us'.

- All human life is of equal worth.

- The individuals who participate in military conflict are sons, daughters, brothers, sisters, fathers, mothers, and neighbors. They are all members of a family and citizens of the world community.

- When we use language as *'terrorist'*, *'rebel'*, *'insurgent'* and other labels like these we depersonalize, dehumanize and objectify these individuals and make their actions less noble and their aspirations less worthy.

- Every human being does the best they can with what they know. No individual intends to make a bad decision or take an action they know is the wrong action. Every individual believes their actions to be the right actions. And from their perspective it is.

- Contrary to political rhetoric God is on the side of both combatants in the battlefield.

- War represents the failure of the human condition to resolve complex human challenges in more reasoned, civilized and respectful ways.

- A disproportionate amount of our Nation's resources (financial, people, ideas) is dedicated to an infrastructure that wages war rather than an infrastructure that supports and encourages peaceful actions and collaborative solutions.

- Most people do not place peace as their highest value; justice, revenge, comfort, wealth, security, power and many other values are consistently placed higher than the value of peace.

One day we will achieve peace, either through the intentional efforts of dedicated and committed leaders and citizens, or through the collective collapse of the human condition due to the ongoing destruction of war. I dedicate my resources to the former.

It is only when we search *within* for the cause of war will we be able to create peace. If we continue to focus our attention on the behaviors of others we will fail to recognize and address our own capacity for behaving in destructive ways.

If peace is to be achieved it must begin with each of us making a commitment to being peaceful. It must begin with each of us leaning the skills and strategies for peaceful decision-making and peaceful conflict resolution.

The battlefield that needs to be won does not exist *outside* of us but rather *inside* of us. Only then will we make progress in our desire for a peaceful world.

Love Not Hate

I've been struggling to hold onto my peace of late. I'm not sure what is behind this renewed struggle. I suspect it has something to do with some the recent events that are occurring in our world.

I felt despair when our major media and political leaders continued to repeat the decade long story of deception with regards to 9/11. Very little attention was given to examining the underlying assumption that the events of that notorious day were caused by a handful of 'terrorists' armed with box-cutters.

And then there was the welcome offered to former US Vice President Dick Cheney by members of Vancouver's elite who chose, quite literally, to walk on the backs of individuals protesting the illegal actions of Cheney during his time in the Bush administration.

I was in shock and awe to see well dressed men and women shelling out $500.00 to hear the words of the self-confessed proponent of torture and other internationally recognized war crimes.

Unfortunately there are countless more examples of violations of human rights, disrespect of the Earth, greed, short sighted and unconscious thinking.

Thus when I sat to consider my message for this month's newsletter I asked the universe to send me some inspiration.

Upon opening my Google search engine I noticed for the first time a link to **'Buddhist Quote of the Day'**. I moved the curser to the link and with a slight tap I was invited to consider these words:

> *"Hatred does not cease through hatred.*
> *Hatred ceases through love."*

Many masters and enlightened beings have given us this same message. Jesus encouraged us to *"Love Thy Enemies"*. It appears to me, however, that most of us do not trust love. We do not have confidence that peace will get us where we want to go.

Just this week a client shared his reluctance to my message of 'peace begins with me'. David articulated his reluctance by stating - *"I'm afraid to become peaceful. My fear is the peacefulness will cause me to be passive and there is too much that needs to be changed to be passive."*

At times I share David's concern. I wonder if the message of love, peace, and forgiveness is enough to create the kind of changes required for humanity to survive. I sent messages of forgiveness to those who pushed past me to honor Mr. Cheney. My forgiveness didn't stop them from forcing their way through the crowd and breaking bread with Mr. Cheney.

I recognize that my challenge is I have a need for change to happen on *my* terms and timeline. This need to have change happen when I want causes me to use judgment, anger, and resentment as a response to ignorance, greed and other forms of unconscious behavior.

I have a few messages of inspiration that serve to re-focus my attention on *my* actions and *my* behaviors as the means to making this world better. One is the message offered by Byron Katie, author of **Loving What Is** (Harmony Books, 2002).

Katie explains there are 'three kinds of business' - *my* business, *your* business, and *God's* business. Katie suggests that when in a challenging situation to ask the question - *"Who's business am I in?"*

The second message is a quote I have posted on my desk at work. The message states: *"Adversity provides me with an opportunity to demonstrate my mastery."* What this means is that without adversity it is impossible for me to demonstrate my mastery over my mind and heart.

Anyone can be loving when those around are loving. The true test of mastery is, *can I be loving in the presence of deception and falsehoods? Can I be loving in the presence of Mr. Cheney and those who support him? Can I be loving in the presence of humans behaving in ways far below their divine potential?*

I'm glad I went to the Cheney protest. It was important for me to express my wish that humans treat each other with more dignity and respect. I only wish I had gone with more love and peace in my heart.

Imagine perceiving the world through Stillness.

You are that power, that goodness, that aliveness,
that Stillness beyond that temporary form
in which you appear for a flash,
a brief time and gone.

And that's the deeper meaning
of the Old Testament saying,

'Be still and know that I am God'.

~ Eckhart Tolle

Love Thy Enemy

It is with some trepidation that I write an article that pertains to the events which occurred in the United States ten years ago this month. While I believe there are important lessons for us to learn and affirm from the events of September 2001, I am also sensitive to the fact that most of us have been inundated with images and rhetoric, and that much of it is designed to evoke as much shock, anger and emotion as possible. It is not my intention to evoke the kind of disturbed feelings normally associated with this event.

However I believe with the benefit of hindsight and perspective, that it is important for us to reflect upon the events of September 2001 and examine our role in what occurred.

Much of the impetus for writing this month's newsletter was stimulated by my re-reading of Eckhart Tolle's 2005 publication - **A New Earth**. In A New Earth Tolle examines the role of the ego and speaks specifically to the activity of war. Tolle declares, *"War is a mind-set."*

Tolle explains, *"There is a deep interrelatedness between your state of consciousness and external reality."*

In other words, the wars that followed the events of September 2001 were *not* caused by the events of the eleventh day of that month. The wars that began with that event and continue to this day are a reflection of the collective unconsciousness of the human society. The wars are the result of the collective dysfunction and insanity of the human mind.

Author Paul Levy in his work, **The Madness of George W. Bush** (AuthorHouse, 2006) writes from the same perspective. Levy introduces his work with the statement, "*If you think this book is about the madness of George W Bush, you will be disappointed. This book is about our collective madness. George W is simply a reflection of our "collective psychosis"*. His rise to power and his ability to enact the kind of decisions made is a reflection of who *we* are.

There were alternatives to war in 2001. I clearly remember the discussion that followed in the wake of September 11th. I remember the voices that encouraged us to use the events of that day as a catalyst to examine the role the United States is playing on the world stage and how their culture and values may have contributed to the purported attack.

Unfortunately, those calling for increased consciousness, for discussion, reflection and examination of personal responsibility were drown out by those calling for armed military intervention, retaliation, and retribution of those perceived to be the attackers.

What Tolle and Levy are speaking to is our cultural norm to go to war. Beyond the external enemy (which has been in existence almost non-stop for the past one hundred years), we have been at war with many things - drugs, crime, poverty, cancer, disease, and terrorism among others. On a more personal level our need to be right causes us to go to war with our neighbors, partners, families and workmates.

The problem with going to war is that we strengthen what ever it is we are fighting against. Tolle writes,

"*Unconsciousness cannot be defeated by attacking it. Even if you defeat your opponent, the unconsciousness will simply have moved into you, or the opponent reappears in a new disguise.*"

We certainly have witnessed the truth of this statement over the past ten years.

The solution is for each of us individually and collectively to examine our own unconscious behaviors. The path out of unconsciousness is to examine and root out those beliefs and attitudes that permit us to do harm to another and to use war as a way to resolve our most complex challenges.

The cause of war is not the 'terrorist'. The cause is our collective unconsciousness. The threat is not *another*. The biggest threat we face is our failure to treat all living beings and species with respect and dignity. The solution will ultimately be found in changing our selves rather than changing the other.

Tolle encourages us to become aware of the forces of fear, anger or hostility as they move through us. To notice when our mind is racing to defend its position, to justify, attack or blame. In other words to acknowledge when there is *something in us* that feels threatened and wants to survive at all costs.

In these moments we need to pause and notice our unconsciousness, then identify with the part of us that notices. *This is our higher self. This is our conscious Being.*

And so, when the images and rhetoric of that eventful day are re-broadcast, as I anticipate they will, it is my hope you not allow yourself to become hijacked emotionally and pulled into an even deeper state of unconsciousness.

Rather, that you use this as an opportunity to move to higher consciousness and awareness of self. We might even consider responding as we were instructed more than two thousand years ago - *"love thy enemy"*.

Standing outside the fire.
Standing outside the fire.
Life is not tried, it is merely survived,
if you're standing outside the fire.

~ Garth Brooks

When Disaster Strikes

We have been inundated over the past week with images, stories and concerns about the earthquake in Japan. It is common to hear friends, family and colleagues passionately engaged in conversation about the latest developments occurring there.

In addition to witnessing the impact of the earthquake and tsunami on the Japanese people I have been observing the impact on people here. It is clear that many people are severely affected by what they are seeing, hearing and imagining is occurring or might occur on distant shores. As I observe the impact these events have on those around me I wonder whether we are well served by our persistent exposure to the world's most tragic events.

There is always some catastrophe, disaster or unfortunate circumstance to capture our interest, concern and attention. If it's not the earthquake in Japan or New Zealand, it's a plane crash, a car accident, an assault, or other story of desperation and despair.

I've learned that my heart is too tender to regularly expose myself to these images and commentary. I become wounded, hurt, scared and angry when I take in the images of tragic events, and at the same time have little or no capacity to respond in any meaningful way to bettering the circumstances or improving the condition of those I'm observing.

In an effort to maintain my peace and joy I've chosen to remove myself from exposure to these images and stories. About ten years ago my family and I made a decision to disconnect cable service and remove the televisions from our home. At the same time I unsubscribed from national and international print media. I restricted my newspaper reading to papers that report the events of my local community.

Some might say I'm sticking my head in the sand; that I'm being an ostrich. The argument could be made that I'm ignoring my responsibility as an international citizen. My mother regularly challenges me on my decision and worries I'll be uninformed should there be some disaster.

My rationale is that I'm restricting my exposure to areas where I have some influence and capacity to effect change. I've learned that to inundate myself with images, stories and speculations where I have no capacity to influence the outcome only serves to overwhelm my emotions and leave me feeling frustrated and powerless.

I've learned there is little I can do to alleviate the suffering in Japan, the turmoil in Libya, or the hardships in Christchurch. And so I prefer to focus my attention on events and circumstances where I can make a difference.

Research into the impact of the bombing of the Murrah Federal Building in Oklahoma City in 1995 provided some interesting insight on the human experience when confronted with a tragedy. When the explosions first occurred many citizens rushed to the site of the demolished building and worked feverishly to remove debris and rubble to release trapped individuals. Eventually the Police, Fire and other first responders arrived at the scene and restricted access to the demolished building. They insisted the average citizen stand on the outside of the yellow tape.

Researchers investigating the impact of the trauma discovered those citizens who first arrived at the scene and had an opportunity to make a contribution to the recovery effort experienced a *lower* level of trauma. However those individuals who arrived later and were restricted to *only watching* the recovery efforts of others were *the most severely* affected by the events of that day. It appears the ability to contribute and make a difference allows us to cope with difficult life events.

With this understanding we might want to re-evaluate the value of regularly exposing ourselves to traumatic events via television, newspapers, You Tube, and other forms of mass media.

I am not suggesting we ignore the plight and hardships of others. Rather, that we be thoughtful and discerning with our exposure to these traumatic images and commentary, and if possible participate in opportunities where we can make a difference in alleviating the suffering of others. And in this way we are all healthier and happier.

When Disaster Strikes – Part Two

I received a number of responses to my last essay - **When Disaster Strikes**. Many people wrote to share they too have reached the conclusion that exposing oneself indiscriminately to images and messages of disaster, destruction and suffering does not serve us well. I also received responses from individuals who chastised me for "sticking my head in the sand" and not caring about others.

I want to clarify that I am not advocating a strategy that ignores the challenges we face in the world. These challenges are significant and need our attention. What I am advocating for is that we respond to these challenges in ways that enable us to move through them and emerge out the other side, rather than be defeated by them.

I witness many people being defeated by the challenges we face. This week I received a phone call from a mother who was in deep despair after viewing the news broadcasts of the difficult circumstances in Japan. The woman was despondent and discouraged. She was imagining a world with high levels of radiation and people dying in great numbers.

And while this exists as a possibility in the future, she was experiencing intense suffering now even though this outcome currently exists only in the realm of possibility and not actuality. In other words her suffering was due to her *imagination* rather than the present *reality*.

In my experience these significant life challenges offer us a choice. We can move into these challenges with the idea of seeing them as evidence of *despair* and *destruction*, or we can see them as tremendous *opportunities*.

Barbara Marx Hubbard, author of the book **Conscious Evolution** (1998) is of the perspective that a crisis is a *'birthing'*. Hubbard invites us to experience a crisis as an opportunity to transform and to engage life in larger and more meaningful ways than lived previously.

In my journey with my son Joshua I experienced his crises in both of these ways. Initially I was devastated by the loss of my son's health and well-being. After a period of time I came to recognize the gift in this experience. My journey with my son was a catalyst in deepening my understanding of patience, acceptance, forgiveness, compassion, love and peace.

My suffering lifted me into a more meaningful and higher quality of life. I now consider these kinds of difficult experiences as *"gifts of darkness"*. I now consider suffering as a gateway to wisdom.

I believe that to make peace with these powerful events we need to accept that there is more to us than our physical bodies; that we exist beyond this physical garment and this present incarnation; that we are more than what is contained between our head and our toes.

Eckhart Tolle teaches that what arises from our suffering is a new consciousness; that we are in the process of becoming *a new species*. Tolle says we ought to be more interested in our *inner state* than the state of the *outside world*.

Barbara Marx Hubbard invites us to see the crisis as a birthing and to use these events as opportunities to *"evolve by choice not by chance"*.

Gregg Braden in his book **Walking Between The Worlds - The Science of Compassion** (1997) shares research that confirms that human emotion determines the actual patterning of DNA within our body. He states that shifting our body chemistry by shifting our viewpoint is perhaps the single most powerful tool we have available to us.

To some these ideas may seem like nonsense. What I know for certain is that we cannot solve the complex challenges we face from a place of fear and despair and thus anything that only adds to our fear and despair is not helpful.

We need to transcend our primitive brain structure that is limited to fight or flight and engage our higher brain that has the capacity to be creative, collaborative, innovative and intuitive and access a universal wisdom.

Let us accept the circumstances we find ourselves in at this moment in our evolution as a species and engage fully in finding solutions. These solutions will require us to live in completely different ways than we are now.

And this is a blessing we should all welcome.

*Those who believe they can do something
and those who believe they can't are both right.*

~ Henry Ford

This Is My Lucky Day

Michael was feeling pretty beaten up. Life was not going according to plan and in spite of his best efforts to remain positive the challenges confronting Michael had gotten the better of him. In his despair Michael gave me a call. *"Ted, I need your help. I can't seem to keep my head above water. I feel like I'm drowning. Everything I touch turns bad."*

This wasn't true. Michael had a long history of overcoming adversity. Michael's father left when he was still an infant, leaving he and his mother in a state of poverty. Michael and his mother spent time homeless, then living in temporary shelters, and eventually government-supported housing.

Michael started working at age thirteen. He knew even then that he needed to take responsibility for his future. Michael set incredibly high expectations for himself. He graduated from high school, attended university, and while there he earned three degrees and the respect of many. Michael was determined to be a multi-millionaire by the time he was forty.

Michael achieved much by the time he reached his fortieth birthday including starting up numerous businesses and receiving high returns on his investment of time, energy and money. But Michael also insisted on playing life as a high risk/high reward game and currently his life was in a down turn. His businesses were struggling, his debts mounting, and his despair growing.

I spent time listening to Michael as he shared his story of despair. When I attempted to shift Michael to a more positive and proactive frame of mind he was having nothing of it. Regardless the words and suggestions I offered Michael was unable to shift his perspective. He kept repeating his mantra over and over again - *"I'm a failure. I'm unlucky. I don't deserve."*

During our session last week I tried something different. I invited Michael to participate in an experiment with me. I asked if he would be willing to consider changing his story. Would he be willing to explore how life might respond to him if he told a different story, presented a different persona, and held a different emotion? I invited Michael to wake up each day for one week and declare to the universe - *"Today is my lucky day."* In his desperation Michael decided to give it a try.

Yesterday I received a telephone call from Michael. He was ecstatic. The joy rippled through the telephone line like a tsunami. *"Ted, you won't believe what's happening to me!"* He then paused and said, *"Well, maybe you will."* Then Michael shared what had occurred since I last spoke with him. *"I did what you asked me to do. Even though I woke up the next day with my normal state of despair and desperation I began our little experiment. I told myself - 'Michael, this is your lucky day'. I have to admit I wasn't feeling lucky but I repeated the phrase over and over again in my mind. I must have repeated it more than one hundred times as I got dressed, ate my breakfast, and drove into the office."*

"When I arrived at the office the telephones were ringing off the hook. My email box was stuffed with emails. My staff was running around like crazy. 'What's going on?'" I asked. "We don't know." they said. "It's been like this all morning." "Ted, I discovered that a reporter had done a very positive article on my company and people

were calling from around the world wanting more information." Michael gushed with enthusiasm. "*Its amazing. I didn't even know the article was being written.*"

"*Congratulations Michael.*" I said.

But Michael wasn't finished. Michael proceeded to tell me that he was scheduled to do a noon hour presentation on his company. After the presentation a gentleman approached him with a check. "*Ted, he put the check in my hand and said he was interested in investing in my company. It was the second biggest check I've seen in my life.*"

"*Wow Michael! That's amazing.*"

"*Ted, I'm not done. On my way home I received a phone call from my realtor. He was calling about a building I bought as an investment a few years ago. The building turned out to be a bad investment and I was loosing money on it. I figured it would take years for me to break even with it. It was another example of how I figured I had failed. The realtor was calling to let me know the value of the building had been re-assessed and was now worth 1.1 million dollars more than I paid for it.*"

"*Ted, this has been the luckiest day of my life!*" exclaimed Michael. "*Thank you for your assistance.*"

"*No, Michael, thank you. You have reminded me once again that amazing things can and do happen in life; that the world doesn't follow a linear progression from A to B to C. Magic can and does happen.*" We both laughed, then Michael said, "*I've got to go. I've got lots to do.*"

May you have an abundance of magic in your life and may today be your lucky day!

*The significant problems we face
cannot be solved at the same level of thinking
we were in when we created them.*

~ Albert Einstein

Complex Problems Cannot Be Solved Alone

I have found the discussion (and I use that term loosely) during the last month of the Canadian Federal election campaign curious. There was much made of the ills of a *'coalition'*. If someone were new to the English language it would be easy to assume a coalition was some kind of dreaded disease that must be avoided at all costs.

Some of Canada's political parties have warned of the dangers of coalitions and advised against supporting anyone who would even consider entering into a coalition. Others have been very assertive in declaring they would never enter into a coalition.

I have to admit I'm confused by this kind of discourse. My confusion is based on my understanding of what the word means. The dictionary informs me that a coalition is *"an alliance for combined action"*.

What I do know is we live in a complex world of competing ideas, values and strategies. I am of the opinion that complex social problems cannot be solved alone; that the challenges we face today requires the collective thoughts, ideas and commitments of a large group of people.

Nature offers us a powerful lesson. Research into the natural world has revealed that *collective wisdom* is more intelligent than *individual wisdom*. I'm told a school of fish, a hive of bees or a flock of birds is fifty times more responsive to its environment than any single fish, bee or bird.

Charles Darwin, who has unfortunately been attributed with the phrase – *"the survival of the fittest"* couldn't have been more misunderstood. Darwin thoroughly understood and documented that the most significant determinant of survival of a species was the capacity of the species *to work together*.

My concern with the recent electioneering and pattern of governance typical in our society today is the tendency to treat others as combatants or enemies rather than as cohorts and collaborators in finding solutions to our most complex social and organizational challenges.

Adam Kahane is a Canadian researcher and facilitator, and author of **Transformative Scenario Planning – Working Together to Change the Future** (2012). Kahane has worked with some of the most intractable social and political challenges of our time. Kahane was invited by President-elect Nelson Mandela to address the huge societal and relational gaps between the blacks and whites in South Africa. Kahane has also worked to ease the Israeli and Palestinian conflicts, as well as conflicts between governments and rebels in many countries around the world.

Kahane believes that collaboration is critical to achieving sustainable solutions. He states that *enduring relationships* are primary to enable us to operate as a single intelligence, and that *'inter-dependence'* not *'independence'* is the outcome we ought to be pursuing.

His observation is that groups, organizations and even countries fail because of their inability to work together. Kahane often responds to the hostility and disregard he witnesses between participants in meetings with the following statement –

"Some of you act as if you have no expectation of a relationship beyond this conversation."

My challenge with the kind of campaigning I am witnessing in this election is that much of the discourse between rivals would invite the comment made by Kahane above. The battering, bruising and disrespect expressed during the campaign would seem to minimize or extinguish any potential of these elected officials to work together in some kind of collaboration after the election.

It is time we demanded that our leaders and elected officials treat each other with respect and dignity; that they acknowledge the need for collaboration and accept that collectively we have a greater capacity to address our social challenges than when we operate as a community of individuals in conflict with one another.

In my mind *an alliance for combined action* is exactly what is needed.

And the LORD said unto Cain,
Where *is* Abel thy brother?
And he said, I know not: *Am* I my brother's keeper?

~ King James Bible

What Will You Choose?

One of the aspects of travel I enjoy is the opportunity to witness other human beings – how they live, what they think, and how they perceive their world. One of my favorite activities is to read the Letters To The Editor of the local newspaper. My journey to Phoenix was no exception. Each day I faithfully scanned the **Arizona Republic** for the opinions and perspectives of those who reside there.

The opinions as expressed on Tuesday, December 14th were especially engaging. The topics of the day included a broad spectrum of issues including - the financial crisis, illegal immigration, the ongoing wars in Iraq and Afghanistan, and the complexities of the evolving medical system in the United States affectionately known as 'Obamacare'.

While the opinions and ideas expressed were similar to those expressed in countless newspapers throughout the country, this particular edition was interesting in how effectively it crystallized the dilemma we face in the world today.

The first letter complimented the newspaper on their recent efforts to explain the challenges presented by the mass immigration of Mexicans into Arizona. The author expressed his appreciation for the comprehensiveness of the paper's review of the issue and then offered his own opinion on how we ought to proceed. He stated:

> *"As long as there are hungry people in this world, and as long as there exist great disparities in the standards of living in neighboring countries, there will be immigration issues.*

Until we as a world address issues of poverty and starvation, all the border patrols and fences and policemen will not stem the flow."

The author concluded with the statement – *"I only wish our politicians would work on making this country and the world a better place for all to live."*

The final letter to the editor that day presented a very different point of view. This author, while speaking specifically to the question of whether the government ought to fund body-organ transplants, was emphatic on the role of government and what it ought to do and not do.

This author opinioned that government has no role in improving the welfare of its citizens. He argued –

"Using the government to force people to pay taxes for the use of other people is theft. This includes using tax funds for body-organ transplants, food stamps, public schools, public libraries, Social Security, Medicare, etc. "

The author concluded with reminding readers of the 8th Commandment – *"Thou shalt not steal."*

These authors typify the challenges and choices that confront each and every one of us today. It is not just governments that must decide how to address matters as immigration, poverty, hunger, homelessness and healthcare. Each of us will need to make a decision on how we will proceed as a community of beings.

Our world is no longer separate and distinct entities, though our size and distance, and our arbitrary labels as distinct Nations give us the illusion of being separate.

The truth is, what we choose, how we live, and what we believe sends out ripples that impact the planet and all who live here.

We no longer have the option to act as if our actions and choices are independent from others. We no longer have the option to avoid making choices. It is now apparent that each of our decisions has global consequences both now and in the future. The choices we make today, the products we buy, the foods we eat, the decisions we make with regards to immigration, wars, healthcare and homelessness have real and lasting impact. It has become abundantly clear that *"what we sow, we reap"*.

My own belief is that we need to adopt an attitude similar to that expressed by the author of the first letter. We need to think about how to make the world a better place for everyone. We need to think about the health of <u>all</u> citizens, not just our friends, families, or Nation. We need to consider all species as brothers and sisters, not just our culture, clan, or local community. We need to be *'our brother's keeper'*.

Until recently the goal in the disability community was to increase the independence of people with a disability. We now know that *in*dependence is not the goal, rather it is *inter*dependence. It is our relationships, not our personal skills or assets that make us happy, healthy and safe. It is not the survival of the *fittest*, but rather the survival of the *community* that needs to be addressed.

*Love without power is sentimental and anemic.
And power without love is reckless and abusive.*

~ Martin Luther King Jr.

Power And Love

Occasionally when I write about peace I am chided on my naivety. The implied message is that peace is passive and even reckless in the face of powerful and destructive forces.

There is truth to this assertion. Adam Kahane, author of **Power and Love** (2010) writes of the impotence of love when it stands alone without power. He quotes Martin Luther King Jr. who stated - *"Love without power is sentimental and anemic. And power without love is reckless and abusive."* The task before us is to combine power and love.

King says -

> *"One of the great problems of history*
> *is that the concepts of love and power*
> *have usually been contrasted as opposites*
> *so that love is identified with the resignation of power,*
> *and power with the denial of love.*
> *It is precisely this collision of immoral power*
> *with powerless morality*
> *which constitutes the major crisis of our time."*

I think King and Kahane have something important for us to consider. In both my personal and professional life I've witnessed the effect that love and power can have when they are out of balance. I lived much of my life with more emphasis on love with the result that I've often experienced anger, resentment and frustration at my own powerlessness.

And I've witnessed the effect that power without sufficient love can and does have on humanity. All wars, conflicts and assaults are a consequence of too much power and not enough love.

So, why is it so difficult to balance love and power?

The reason is we have not been taught how to balance power and love. Many of us have abandoned our power, either through witnessing the destructive results of power and not wishing to align with it, or being convinced by our media, religions and political leaders that we really have no power anyways.

And when we love, our love is often narrow and conditional. Most of us love only a small group of people - family, extended family, race, religion, culture, or Nationality. This places the majority of humanity on the *outside* of our love. In addition, we love others while they are nice and loving and respond in unloving ways when the other fails to meet our expectations.

Upon reading Kahane's Power and Love I've identified five actions we might want to consider if we wish to improve the condition of humanity on the planet.

1. Claim our Power

Recognize that we are powerful beings and have the *capacity* to act. More than having the capacity to act, we have the *responsibility* to act. Claiming our power means shifting from *"someone should"* to *"I will"*.

It means recognizing that life is a result of the choices <u>we</u> have made individually and collectively, and owning our responsibility for choosing better. Our capacity to address our toughest social challenges depends on our willingness to admit that we are part of the problem.

"If you are not part of the problem,
then you can't be part of the solution."
~ Professor Bill Tolbert

2. Expand Our Love

We need to expand our love to include everyone - no boundaries, borders, limits or conditions. All boundaries and borders are artificial and man made. It is our perceived separateness that allows us to cause harm to another. All wars begin with a distancing and objectification of the other so that harming them is justified. To solve today's challenges everyone must be valued and uplifted.

3. Build Our Capacity for Co-Creation

One of the discoveries from nature is that collective intelligence is higher than individual intelligence. Scientist have discovered that a hive of bees, a school of fish, and a flock of birds is fifty times more responsive to their environment that any individual bee, fish or bird. The same is true for us. Group intelligence is always higher than individual intelligence.

"If you want to walk fast, walk alone.
If you want to walk far, walk together."
~ African proverb

4. Manage Our Fear

The root cause of man's destructive behavior is fear. Fear is a consequence of living in an imagined future and telling oneself a negative story. I've learned we can always manage _this_ moment. What we can't manage is the fear caused by our imagination about what _might_ happen. Fear activates our reptilian brain, which is only concerned with 'fight or flight'.

To solve today's complex social problems we need to activate our higher brain, which is able to be creative, intuitive and collaborative.

> _"Power over happens when our fear of being hurt exceeds our fear of hurting others."_

5. Refuse to Choose Between Power And Love

Choosing either power or love is destructive. There is no future in either power _or_ love, only in power _and_ love. When we choose love or power we inevitably re-create the existing reality or worse. Power is never absent, only concealed. Concealed power is harder to deal with than overt power. Love without power deceitfully reinforces the status quo.

It is time to end immoral power and powerless morality. It is time for change. More of the same will only lead to further destruction and the end of life as we know it.

The Delusions of War

I've pondered about this ongoing relationship humanity has with war and our support for it. I've wondered why is it that we cannot seem to behave in more reasoned and civilized ways. I've questioned why it is considered naïve and unrealistic to request that we respond to the challenges and differences we face with *diplomacy* and *compassion* rather that weapons and destruction.

I acknowledge that war has been a part of humanity from the beginning. The amount of time in recorded history that humans have been at peace, where no country has taken up arms against another, is measured in days and months rather than years, decades or centuries.

The behavior of the United States in invading and occupying Iraq and Afghanistan, for example, isn't new or isolated. The United States has invaded and overthrown fourteen governments over a 110-year period beginning with the Hawaiian monarchy in 1893.

My perspective is that the real issue is not about *remembering* or *forgetting* but rather about seeing through the delusions that cause us to view war in such noble and patriotic wrappings. With very few exceptions war is done for ideological, political and economic gain.

War is about controlling valuable resources, strategic locations, or imposing one's will upon another as a way of intimidating other potential competitors. *Why don't we see this fact more clearly? Why are we so easily seduced into believing that war is necessary, justified, noble, and unavoidable?*

In the build up to the invasions of Iraq and Afghanistan I watched how the enemy was depersonalized, dehumanized and objectified. Those men and women in Afghanistan who so valiantly fought against the Soviet occupation were no longer referred to as *freedom fighters* or *resistors*. Now they were *terrorists, extremists,* and *members of the axis of evil.*

While it is easy to sit in judgment of the decisions and actions of the US, British and Canadian governments I am more interested in reflecting on how this path became a viable option in the first place. How is it that decent and caring citizens were convinced that aggressive military action of such scale and destruction was a good idea?

We can blame Mr. Bush and his cohorts in Washington who insisted that war was the only option. We can blame the media for failing to ask tough questions in the lead up to the invasion. We can blame Saddam for his leadership practices in Iraq. We can blame Afghanistan for insisting that Bin Laden be tried by an International court rather than a US court.

We would be better served by considering how the insanity of Mr. Bush and others is a reflection *of our own insanity.* How the failure of the media to ask tough questions is a reflection of our own unwillingness to ask tough questions. How the stories that are told to us about war is a reflection of our own willingness to accept these stories.

It is only when we search *within* for the cause of such behavior that we will be able to heal ourselves and create peace.

If we continue to focus on the actions and behavior of others we will fail to recognize and address our own capacity for behaving badly.

The good news is the delusions of war are beginning to disintegrate. The Canadian publication **Peace** recently announced a number of notable achievements that are worthy of celebrating:

- In July 2010 the Canadian Federal Court of Appeal issued its unanimous judgment that the Canadian Government's rejection of Iraq war resister Jeremy Hinzman's application for permanent residence in Canada was *"flawed and unreasonable"*.

- More than 4,037 mayors in 144 countries have joined a campaign to eliminate nuclear weapons by 2020.

- This year's annual survey of public opinion conducted by the German Marshall Fund discovered that only two countries, United States and Britain, have more than 50% of its citizens in agreement with the statement - *"Under some conditions war is necessary to obtain justice."*

Maybe we are beginning to see through the delusions of war. Maybe peace is being increasingly embraced as realistic, necessary and possible. Maybe soon we will organize events to remember war because it no longer exists.

I'm starting with the man in the mirror.
I'm asking him to change his ways.

~ Michael Jackson,
Man in the Mirror

Man In The Mirror

I've been traveling the last four weeks. I've been fortunate to spend time in both Australia and New Zealand. Visiting distant places provides an opportunity to reflect on the things I take for granted. It also offers an opportunity to recognize our differences and similarities in how we live on this planet.

The lessons received were more than learning to drive on the left side of the road, shift gears with my left hand, or choosing between a 'tall black' or a 'flat white' coffee in the mornings.

My reason for traveling was to participate in two disability conferences. My intention was to share the message that everyone, especially individuals with a disability, have something valuable to offer. Through presentations as *'The Hidden Gifts of Disability'* and *'How Disability Saved the World'* my goal was to deepen awareness of the contributions those with differing abilities can and do make.

I shared the story of when my son attended grade seven at a local school and was intentionally selected by his teacher to be a member of his class because Jeff recognized that other children were kinder and gentler when around Josh. Jeff's thinking was that having Josh in his class would make it a kinder and gentler place for all children to learn. As I shared my story others came forward to share the gifts they had received from having a child with disabilities.

One mother talked of how her non-disabled child became a strong social justice advocate as a result of witnessing how others treated his sibling. Another parent began her story with the words, "*My teacher is twelve years old.*" This parent explained that her daughter of twelve has been a profound source of wisdom in her life.

Another mother began by telling us that she has two special children, rather than two children with special needs. A colleague disclosed that her attraction to working in the disability field is because she feels unconditionally accepted by those she supports.

What I discovered in my travels is that in spite of the distance and differences there is a common desire amongst all human beings to belong, to be included, to be valued and to contribute. What the disability community offers is an opportunity to recognize our similarities even though we may appear outwardly as different.

What I also noticed is a pattern that concerned me. I notice that many people look to others to be the agents of inclusion, acceptance, belonging, and change rather than recognizing we *all* have the ability and the responsibility to include, accept, invite, and change our communities.

The fact is our communities are a shared creation by those of us who live in them. Our way of living is the result of our collective thoughts and actions. Rather than perceive another as the leader or agent of change, it is imperative that we recognize that each of us has the capacity as well as the responsibility for deciding how we share the spaces and resources of this planet.

One of the more powerful experiences of my journey was the in-flight movie. The film was the documentary **This Is It**. The film captures the rehearsals for the concert Michael Jackson was producing prior to his untimely death.

In the documentary Jackson speaks directly to the camera and says –

> *"This is it. If we want change, it's up to us."*

A song of Jackson's that impacted me deeply is **Man in the Mirror**. These lyrics say it all:

> *"I'm gonna make a change for once in my life.*
> *Gonna make a difference.*
> *Gonna make it right.*
> *I'm starting with the man in the mirror.*
> *I'm asking him to change his ways.*
> *And no message could have been any clearer.*
> *If you wanna make the world a better place,*
> *Take a look at yourself and then make a change."*

I witness a profound transformation occurring. Greater numbers of individuals are recognizing the need to foster belonging, inclusion, respect and dignity regardless of differences in ability, culture, religion or status.

And while the families in the disability community might be more sensitive to the issues of belonging and inclusion, we all benefit when humanity learns to accept and value everyone unconditionally.

It is possible that the efforts of the disability community to promote belonging and inclusion will save the world for all of us.

Beyond Hope

Last weekend I experienced an opportunity to face some adversity. In the grand scheme what occurred was nothing. But in the moment the change in plans was unsettling.

My plan was to visit my brother Tom and his family at his beautiful Kelowna home. The weather was hot and sunny and my mind was filled with joyful stories of relaxing on the beach with a cold refreshment, engaging in a friendly game of tennis, and participating in stimulating conversations in the shade of his back yard.

I woke early on Saturday, packed a few belongings, snacks and refreshments, and was on my way. It was a gorgeous day. The sun was up, the sky was blue, and the traffic was light. I put on my favorite music, slid open the sunroof and clicked on the cruise control. Life was good.

About forty kilometers east of Hope the 'check engine' light flashed on. Then the temperature gauge began to fluctuate wildly. Within a few minutes the needle on the gauge was firmly buried in the red zone and steam was pouring out of both sides of my engine compartment. I pulled over as quickly as I could. The car sputtered, then stopped.

I opened the hood and peered inside. Steam billowed out as the overflowing radiator spilled onto the hot engine. I refilled the radiator and jumped back inside. The car started but the grinding noises coming from under the hood indicated the problem was more serious. It would appear the water pump had decided this was the time to make its transition.

Undeterred I pulled out my cell phone and punched in directory assistance. When the call repeatedly failed I took a closer look at my phone's display. No cell signal. I could feel my disappointment rising as the reality of my situation began to sink in. It was less and less likely I would be spending the day on the beach or tennis court. I felt a momentary pang of anger. *"Why here, why now?" "What had I done to deserve this?"* I could feel my mind searching for an explanation.

Within moments the light of consciousness began to shine through. I started to *witness* myself and the stories I was authoring in that moment. And as I became conscious of my storytelling and the resulting emotions I began to laugh. How quickly that monkey mind grabs hold! How easy it is to move into blame, shame, and judgment.

I noticed that in this moment I was fine. No real harm had come to me. It was still a beautiful day. All that happened was that my story about what I thought would unfold had been changed. It took me a moment to release the story of how the day *could* have gone and make peace with the day I was *having*.

I stuck out my thumb. Within minutes a car slowed and pulled over. *"Its not a lift I need"* I explained to the driver and his wife. *"I simply need a tow truck and I'm out of cell phone range."* The couple promised to make the call and wished me a good rest of my day.

I took their advice. I pulled a book out of my pack, sat down in the shade of a tree and immersed myself in the beauty of the moment. And I smiled knowing that I had stared into the face of some adversity and come through with grace and ease. All it took was a little acceptance and a decision to make the most of the choices in front of me now.

Ask And It Is Given

Last month I shared my journey of making peace with my day after my car broke down. This experience was a perfect opportunity to demonstrate mastery over my mental and emotional bodies. There is more to the story.

The evening prior to my trip to Kelowna I shared a meal with close friends. At one point during the evening the conversation shifted to the 'ultimate fighting competition' to be held the following day in Vancouver. Ultimate Fighting is a newly evolving sport where combatants face one another in an octagonal cage and are permitted to use any tactic or strategy to overpower their opponent.

Each of us lamented at the crude brutality of the event. We freely opinioned on the kind of person who would attend such an event. Most of our comments were judgmental, derogatory, and dismissive. The conversation might easily have been summed up by Eckhart Tolle's expression – *"We've arrived (at higher consciousness). Sorry that you haven't."*

The next day was the day I shared in my last essay – traveling to Kelowna, sunroof open, sun shining, my favorite music playing and then the 'check engine' light coming on. About one hour after I flagged down a passing motorist a tow truck arrived. My car was winched onto the flat bed and we headed back to Hope. The tow truck operator delivered me to a small, one-man repair shop on the edge of town.

As I stood at the entrance of the garage and peered inside the dim and dirty workplace I noticed a man with well-worn hands and grease smeared across face. His large forearms were poking and prodding the bowels of a large truck raised on the hoist. Hanging on each side of the pick-up's four corners were large, oversized wheels. Anxiously peering under the vehicle was a young man.

What I gathered from their conversation is the young man had just invested many thousands of his hard earned dollars in a new transmission only to notice fluid spewing out the back of his vehicle on its maiden voyage. Disheartened and discouraged he drove his truck into this very same shop to have the source of the leak located and repaired.

The young man and I shared a common bond. We were both at the mercy of this unknown mechanic. The bond of our shared experience drew us together. The young man shared with me his frustration at having only just picked up his vehicle that morning from the transmission specialist. His added concern is that he would miss his intended rendezvous with a friend in Vancouver. *"What takes you to Vancouver?"* I inquired. *"My buddy and I are off to the 'ultimate fighting competition"* he replied.

I laughed inwardly at the synchronicity of the universe, hearing my own judgments reflected back in my mind from the previous evening's conversation. It was not lost on me that I had declared, more a statement than genuine curiosity, *"What kind of person would go to the UFC event?"* Well the universe decided to answer my question.

Eventually the mechanic performed his magic and the monster truck was ready to return to the highway. While the young man cleaned himself up I consulted with the mechanic on the status of my own fate. The mechanic explained there were no parts available in this small town to repair my vehicle. It would take a few days before the repairs could be completed. The good news was the young man's truck was repaired and he was headed to the fighting venue, which is located two blocks from my home. I ran to the driver's side window and asked the young man if he would give me a lift back to Vancouver.

During our two-hour journey together I decided to wade into the topic of the previous evening's conversation. With as much neutrality as I could muster I inquired - *"What motivates you to attend this event?"*. The young man shared the following story:

"My best friend is in Vancouver. He's being cared for in an extended care facility. Two months ago we were swimming at a local lake and my friend dived into an area that was too shallow. The impact with the ground caused a severing of his spinal cord. He's paralyzed from the neck down" the young man explained wiping tears from his eyes. *"I haven't seen him since the accident. I called him and said I wanted to visit him, and asked what he would like to do while I was there. It was his wish to attend the ultimate fighting competition."*

I was struck silent by the power and yet tenderness of the young man's story. And in a moment all of my judgments and assumptions about the kind of person who would attend such an event were shattered. It wasn't the violence and crassness of the competition he desired. It was his desire to honor the request of his wounded friend.

The universe had skillfully reflected back to me a mirror of my own unconsciousness and lack of compassion; my own violence and crassness. And in that moment I was grateful for this lesson in my journey to become a consistently loving and peaceful human being.

Resistance is futile.

~ The Borg (Star Trek)

Nothing Happened

One of my biggest challenges has been to accept reality. I spent much of my adulthood carrying around a story that things ought to be different than they are. When accidents happened, illnesses occurred, and when people made decisions that went against my idea of what is right, I responded with - "*That should never have happened.*" The result is I lived much of my life in anger, frustration and resentment.

In my journey with my son I was challenged to accept reality; to *accept what is.* Eckhart Tolle is the spiritual teacher who brought to my awareness the idea that '*resistance is insanity*'. Resistance doesn't change the event that I'm resisting because the event has already occurred. Instead my resistance changes me into someone who is angry, frustrated and discouraged. Because of my desire to live peacefully and joyfully I needed to learn to accept reality.

When I share this hard earned wisdom in my counseling I'm often asked for a tool or strategy to assist one to accept reality. One of the more effective tools I have utilized over the last few years is a strategy I learned from my wife Darlene. Whenever something unexpected would happen - a dropped dish, spilled milk, a sink overflowing, a scratch on the car, Darlene would respond with the expression, "*Nothing happened*".

The simplicity of this strategy is what makes it so effective. What Darlene's phrase does is remind me that in the grand scheme of life, the dropped dish, the spilled milk, or the sink overflowing is really nothing. And if it's nothing, there is no reason to move into anger or frustration.

In Tolle's latest book **A New Earth**, Tolle shares the story of a woman diagnosed with terminal cancer. Tolle visited the woman regularly to assist her in coping with her medical condition. During one of the visits Tolle arrived to find the woman in a state of great distress.

The woman reported that the cause of her distress was because a ring that had great monetary and sentimental value had gone missing. The woman was certain the individual caring for her had taken it.

Tolle's response was to ask the woman a few simple questions.

> *"Do you realize that you will have to let go of the ring at some point, perhaps quite soon?"*

> *"Will you become less of a person when you let go of the ring?"*

> *"Has who you are become diminished by the loss of the ring?"*

Through Tolle's questions and the woman's willingness to reflect deeply upon the answers the woman came to recognize that she was not diminished by the loss of the ring. She was the same person as before. In addition the woman recognized that her anger and suffering was the result of thinking that her identity was tied to the possession of an object. These questions were Tolle's way of saying "nothing happened".

I've come to recognize that much of my suffering has been the result of allowing my happiness to be tied to things being a particular way. I held on to stories and expectations that in the grand scheme of things were really 'nothing'.

By learning to see the *'nothingness'* of these material possessions, by learning to see the *'nothingness'* of insisting life show up in a particular way I have been able to hold onto my peace and joy more easily.

A colleague of mine who is regularly hired to consult with corporations often uses the following quote when assisting these businesses to stay focused on their goals. Ross states - *"If everything is important, then nothing is important."* His message is that in order to be successful we need to discern what is important from what is not important.

While Ross's statement has profound wisdom, I like the simplicity and the grace that is expressed with my wife's expression - *"Nothing happened."* Try it the next time someone steps outside of your story of what should or shouldn't happen - when a dish gets dropped, a drink spilled, a child comes home with dirt on their clothes, a colleague makes a mistake, or a partner disappoints.

What is important is to hold on to our peace and joy regardless of what life offers.

Our deepest fear is not that we are inadequate.
Our deepest fear is that we are powerful beyond measure.

It is our light, not our darkness, that most frightens us.
We ask ourselves, who am I to be brilliant, gorgeous,
talented, and fabulous? Actually, who are you not to be?

You are a child of God. Your playing small doesn't serve
the world. There's nothing enlightened about shrinking so
that other people won't feel insecure around you. We are
all meant to shine, as children do. We are born to make
manifest the glory of God that is within us.

It's not just in some of us, it's in everyone. And as we let
our own light shine, we unconsciously give other people
permission to do the same. As we are liberated from our
own fear, our presence automatically liberates others.

~ Marianne Williamson

What Do You Do?

Recently I met someone for coffee. Tim was a new acquaintance and therefore one of his first questions was, *"What do you do?"* A standard greeting when meeting someone for the first time.

I gave my standard response - *"I'm a psychotherapist in private practice. I facilitate workshops for organizations and corporations. And I'm an author."* Though I've given this response hundreds of times, this time my answer felt hollow. Something didn't feel right, but I wasn't sure what I was sensing at that moment.

A few days later I heard a story that had a profound impact on me. It's the story of a church official in the 12th century A.D. who was inspecting a new church that was under construction. The building was to be a magnificent structure with multiple towers and steeples, beautiful colored glass windows, and numerous finely crafted statues and sculptures along with other works of art. It was to be the kind of cathedral that takes more than a century to build and where all of the workmen and artisans who began the construction would be long deceased when the building was completed.

The story captures a series of conversations the Bishop had as he toured the work site. His first conversation was with a stonemason. *"What are you doing?"* he asks the mason. *"I'm trimming this block of stone to fit into that wall over there."*

A while later the Bishop speaks with a carpenter. *"What are you doing?"* the Bishop inquires. *"I'm making a door"* answers the wood craftsman. Finally the Bishop sits down to speak with an old man who is carefully sweeping up the debris from the day's activities. *"What are you doing?"* asks the Bishop. *"I'm building a cathedral"* answers the janitor.

How do you respond when asked, "What do you do?" What is your answer? Do you share your greatest vision and own your contribution toward this vision? Or are you seeing only the task in front of you? Are you connected to your higher purpose, or is your life mostly about putting one foot in front of the other? Are you living a life filled with meaning, or a life full of drudgery and frustration?

The janitor recognized that even in the simplest of tasks he was making a contribution toward the building of a great cathedral.

I meet many individuals who have worked their whole lives to support a corporate or business agenda. Many are now wondering about *their* purpose in life. They recognize that working for financial compensation alone is not enough to sustain us. More is required to live a rich life.

What I know is that without a clear sense of our higher purpose the day-to-day tasks lose their meaning with the result that we lose our passion for life.

I wonder how our world might be different if when asked, *"What do you do?"* we responded with a clear declaration of our higher purpose and a vivid description of our own cathedrals? I'm confident answering in this way would lift and inspire those around us to discover and declare their higher purpose too.

Creating Gold

The 2010 Winter Olympic Games are finished. Along with hundreds of thousands of others I was fortunate to witness this two-week extravaganza first hand and to immerse myself fully in the Olympic experience. Not only did I get to marvel at the ability of the human spirit to excel at their chosen endeavor, I enjoyed the companionship of the world's citizens coming together in peace and harmony. My heart was lifted by the sharing of deep emotions ranging from laughter and joy to intense grief and loss.

For me the most powerful event of the Olympic experience wasn't part of the planned schedule. Rather it was one of those experiences that are a by-product of a highly visible international affair. The event that had a deep impact upon me was the anti-Olympic protest that occurred on Day One.

Thousands of individuals filled the streets of Vancouver to express their dissatisfaction with the values and priorities the games represented. Their message was their wish that the world's resources had been spent on other dreams and directed toward other needs of the human condition.

I have compassion for these individuals who felt a sense of frustration and resentment with the Olympic dream. Some of these individuals are champions in their own right offering a high level of commitment to creating a world where humanity lives in harmony and dignity with one another.

My sense of compassion and admiration did not extend however to those protesters who chose to behave in ways that undermined the safety, joy and harmony of others. In particular I did not support those individuals whose actions were primarily focused on *destruction* rather than *creation* and who chose to be *disguised* rather than *open* and *transparent*.

One of the lessons I've gathered from reviewing culture-changing events is that all significant human transformations achieved success because of the power of the *ideas* they promoted and the *integrity* with which they were presented. Their actions were directed toward creating something new and better rather than on attacking and destroying what they disagreed with.

Mahatma Gandhi and Martin Luther King succeeded in transforming our society and our consciousness, not by being *against* something but rather because they were *for* something even bigger. Their actions were respectful, open and creative rather than aggressive, secretive and destructive. And though they made a commitment to non-violence they were clearly not passive or powerless. Their actions were active, intentional, firm and powerful.

David Hawkins, author of **Power vs. Force** (2004) makes a distinction between '*power*' and '*force*'. Much of what we witness in the world today are demonstrations of humans creating change by force.

The regime change in Iraq or the intended modernization of Afghanistan is being done through the efforts of *force* rather than the effects of *power*. True power does not require force.

Gandhi had no military to force the liberation of India from colonial rule. What he had was the power of an idea. So too, King did not use guns and bombs to force the civil rights consciousness upon the United States. Rather King used the power of words and images. King's *I Have A Dream* speech offered words and ideals that transformed a Nation.

The gold medal I took away from the 2010 Olympic experience is the reminder that if I want to transform and transcend mankind's current beliefs, priorities and ways of being in the world I must evoke this change through the inspirational power of *high ideals* and the offer of a *grander vision* rather than through the use of negativity, judgment or other destructive forces which only serve to bring out the worst of humanity.

I hope your Olympic experience enabled you to experience golden moments as well.

To reassert and strengthen moral values
is the duty of everyone,
but it should not be done in hatred or anger.

The true battle is in each and everyone one of us
is being able to view the other side as fellow human beings
while continuing to push for the return of peace
and ethics to society.

~ Phra Phaisan Visalo, Peace advocate

Is This Racism?

Recently a friend forwarded an email he had received and asked my perspective on its contents. The email expressed great concern with a minority group that is increasing its presence in the community. The author of the email stated this minority group is *"unwilling to integrate into mainstream society, settles into enclaves, and holds values and beliefs that are inconsistent with the community in which they have settled"*. The author concludes his email with a plea for us to be *less* tolerant, *less* generous, and *less* welcoming to this and other minority groups.

My friend forwarded the email with the question, *"Is this racist?"* He felt compelled to consider the implications of forwarding an email such as this to others. At the same time he was concerned by the anxious and fearful tone the email had evoked. I appreciated my friend's deep desire to determine what action of his would do the most good.

I joined the discussion my friend's email had inspired. One respondent reminded us that similar sentiments have been expressed for generations whenever a new group of immigrants makes its way to our shores. It wasn't that many years ago that the focus of such concern was directed at Chinese and other Asian migrants. In the community I grew up in similar concerns were raised about the increasing number of Polish, African, Caribbean, East Indian and even Newfoundlanders who were making the community home.

In many cases broad and sweeping statements are made in these situations with the effect that we no longer consider these people as individuals but rather as one homogenous group. Implicit in the statements is that all of these people act the same, hold the same beliefs, and represent the same level of risk to our safety and well being.

It is this broad and all encompassing classification of individuals, cultures and faith groups that invites the question of racism. When we treat others based on some *preconceived* notion of who they are, or pre-judge all of them based on the actions of a few, we are at risk of doing great harm in spite of our intention to do good. The fact is we are all capable of behaving in good and bad ways. We are all capable of expressing the full range of human behaviors.

Where I believe we get lost in our journey to do good is when we focus our attention on what *others* need to do in order to be good citizens. It seems when the focus of concern is directed at others we become distracted from placing our energy and attention where it can have the greatest potential to do good – *one self.*

My friend's email reminds me of the story of the traveler who drives into a small town. The traveler inquires of an elder whom he meets, *"What kind of people live here?"* The elder responds with a question of his own, *"What kind of people live in the town where you come from?"* The stranger answers, *"Oh, they are lazy and irresponsible and fight all the time."* The elder replies, *"The same kind of folk live here as well."*

A little while later another traveler drives into the same town and engages the same elder. *"What kind of people live in this town? The elder gives the same response - "What kind of people live in the town where you come from?"*

The second traveler replies, *"They are happy and loving and very generous."* The elder replies, *"The same kind of folk live here as well."*

The moral of the story is that our perception is more often a statement about our self than it is about others. I think a better focus is not on how *others* are living, but rather on how *I* am living.

Am I living honestly, respectfully, compassionately, open hearted and peacefully?

Am I the kind of citizen and neighbor I would want to live next to?

Am I considerate of differences?

Do I live responsibly?

Our greatest power is in managing our own thoughts and behaviors rather than trying to manage the thoughts and behaviors of others. When we focus on what others need to do different we can be blind to our own misdemeanors.

Byron Katie, author of **Loving What Is** (2002) offers a beautiful piece of wisdom for our consideration. She states:

"There are three kinds of business in this world - my business, your business, and God's business. When in any difficult situation the first question we ought to ask is, "Whose business am I in?"

The perception of power as external splinters the psyche,
whether it is the psyche of the individual,
the community, the nation, or the world.

There is no difference between acute schizophrenia
and a world at war.

~ Gary Zukav, Author
The Seat of the Soul

Peace Is Not A Dream

Like many I celebrated when Barrack Obama succeeded in winning the US Presidential election in November 2008. I was inspired by the powerful words of this presidential candidate. I was lifted by his message of hope that we could resolve the challenges we face as a global community in more collaborative and constructive ways. I was especially moved when Mr. Obama declared during his acceptance speech - *"I will listen to you especially when we disagree."*

As of January 2010 President Obama has had almost a full year to bring a new way of thinking and working to the US government and by extension to the world. I don't think I'm alone in my disappointment as to what President Obama has and has not accomplished during his first year in office.

The wars in Iraq and Afghanistan continue with no end in sight. And rather than end or reduce the US military involvement in the Middle East Obama has increased the number of US solders in Afghanistan to three times the level of the previous administration.

Guantánamo Bay remains open. And while plans have been drafted to close this infamous facility, the intention is to transfer these long-held detainees to another facility in the US where international agreements pertaining to the treatment of prisoners of war will continue to be ignored.

More disconcerting for me is Obama's acceptance of the 2009 Nobel Peace prize.

By accepting the prize, even as he increased the size of the US military presence in the Middle East, Obama showed disrespect to the Nobel Prize itself and to previous Nobel laureates who so clearly demonstrated the need to achieve peaceful ends through peaceful means.

Mr. Obama disregarded the profound teachings and dedication of Mahatma Gandhi, Nelson Mandela and Martin Luther King. Instead he continued to espouse the belief that peace can be achieved through violence.

With more consideration I should not have been surprised by the actions of President Obama. Mr. Obama is a reflection of the *collective* consciousness. While there is increasing discomfort with the mounting fatalities in the current wars, there is not a definitive demand to end these wars as occurred with the ending of the US war in Vietnam.

I acknowledge I have been irresponsible in my desire for peace. I have looked to Mr. Obama to do something that I need to take responsibility for. I have relied too heavily upon Mr. Obama to create peace.

Maybe it's better that Mr. Obama didn't decide to end the wars in the Middle East as he received his Nobel prize because had he done so I and others would not have shared in the responsibility for creating peace; we would not have owned the accomplishment of achieving peace. His action might have again supported the idea that peace is the result of *someone else* behaving different.

Peace needs to be an *individual* decision, an *individual* commitment, and an *individual* responsibility. Anything less will not bring lasting peace. Costa Rica's Nobel Prize winning President, Oscar Arias Sanchez, has it right when he says -

"Peace is not a dream. It is an arduous task.
We must start by finding peaceful solutions to everyday conflicts
with the people around us.
Peace does not begin with the other person;
it begins with each and every one of us."

Peace begins with an individual decision and an individual commitment to behave in peaceful ways - to treat others with respect and dignity; to use peaceful language; to address differences and difficulties collaboratively and constructively; and to refuse to participate in war or in actions that support war.

Peace is about monitoring ones thoughts, words and actions and showing up peacefully in each and every moment regardless how the other person behaves. It is easy to be peaceful when one is surrounded by peace. The true test of *mastery* is to be peaceful when those around us are not.

I learned something else from Mr. Obama this year. I developed an appreciation for the limitations of hope. While hope is vital and even inspiring, hope is not enough. When the opportunity presents itself we must do more than hope. Achieving peace requires action. Living in peace requires that each one of us move from hope into action and behave in peaceful ways.

Peace requires making a choice. It is a choice no one can make for me. I have to choose peace myself. I cannot choose peace for another. Only they can choose peace for themselves. Peace cannot be imposed upon another. Any peace that is imposed by force is not peace but compliance.

I can choose peace regardless whether you choose peace because my peace is not dependent on your peace. However my commitment to peace has the potential to inspire your commitment to peace.

It is no longer good enough to cry peace.
We must act peace, live peace,
and march in peace
in alliance with the people of the world.

~ Chief Shenandoah,
Six Nations Iroquois Confederacy

What 's With All the Talk About Peace?

Recently a friend gently chided me with - *"What's with all this talk about peace? How could we not be peaceful? Unlike many places in the world we don't fear being bombed or shot at. Our dilemma is not whether we will eat but where we will eat. And with the rare exception we go to bed each night expecting to wake in the morning."*

It's true. Our quest to experience peace is, for the most part, not about changing our *external* world. We are blessed with abundance - food, shelter, security and opportunity that exceeds what kings and queens experienced just a century ago. To achieve the peace we desire requires changes to our *internal* world.

Most of the drama and suffering we experience is created in our minds. The demons that need to be slain do not exist outside of us but rather inside of us. Our fear is largely the result of an imagination that regularly manufacturers its own nightmares. Research indicates that the average North American thinks *nine* times as many negative thoughts as positive thoughts.

I know what it is like to have a mind that creates suffering and drama. I lived for years in a chronic state of fear. I regularly imagined dangers and events that never materialized yet suffered nevertheless. I was in a constant state of anxiety and foreboding about the future. That was before I discovered the importance of managing the stories I told myself.

If peace is to be achieved it must begin with each individual making a commitment to being peaceful regardless of what the world offers. The battlefield that needs to be won is the one that exists between the *'events of life'* and *'the meaning we assign to these events'*. Only when we develop mastery over our thoughts and related emotions will we make progress in our desire for a peaceful world.

Ronald Wright, author of **What is America?** (2008), describes America's free fall into fear since September 2001. He is very clear that the current wars in Iraq and Afghanistan weren't caused by a handful of supposed hijackers. Rather, the military invasions and the numerous violations of civil rights and freedoms, international laws and human decency were the result of our *response* to the events of September 2001. It was the *stories* we told ourselves and the *meaning* we assigned to those life events that created these disastrous effects.

When we attribute our thoughts, emotions and actions to the behavior of others we give away one of our most cherished attributes - *the capacity for choice*. I often hear people declare that *someone made them happy, sad, or angry*. When we believe that others are responsible for our emotions and actions we act as if there is no space between *stimulus* and *response*, between *life* and our *response* to life; that our actions are not our doing. It is impossible to create a peaceful world if we declare we are not responsible for our actions.

This week a client eagerly shared his delight in his own progress toward developing mastery over his mental and emotional states. *"Ted"*, he stated joyfully, *"You would be proud of me. On my way here today another driver didn't properly check before changing lanes and scraped the side of my car. A week ago I would have lost it and let him know in no uncertain terms how poor a driver he is. Instead I held onto my peace and my joy. I refused to let this event knock me over. Instead I let him know that nothing important happened. Everything can be fixed and not to worry."*

It is easy to be peaceful when the world around us is peaceful. The real test of mastery is whether we can maintain our peace and our joy when those around us are not peaceful and not joyful. As long as we act as if we are not responsible for our response to life, as long as we make others responsible for our actions and reactions, we will never become a civilized species.

Ronald Wright saves his most important comment for the very last sentence of his book. He writes –

> *"For civilization to continue, we must civilize ourselves."*

We are disturbed not by what happens to us,
but by our thoughts about what happens.

~ Epictetus
Greek Philosopher

Faith or Fear?

Recently I picked up the novel by Kathleen McGowan entitled **The Book of Love** (2009). It's a fictional account of the life and times of the closest followers of Jesus during the first millennium. At one point in the story the heroine is confronted by a mob of angry men who threaten her life. At the pinnacle of the confrontation the heroine receives a Divine message. The angelic messenger declares, "*Fear and faith cannot exist in the same place at the same time. Choose one.*"

It strikes me that we too need to make this choice. We are in a time of accelerated change. The world as we know it is being transformed - economically, environmentally and personally. The paradigms, structures and beliefs that guided us in the past are being challenged. New ways of thinking and living are required. More of the same will not work. But underneath all of the choices is one consistent choice - *faith or fear*?

We might not recognize this is the choice being demanded of us. This is especially true if we associate the word '*faith*' with being aligned with a particular religion. I see the question of faith as larger than which religion will I adhere to. I see faith as the position I take with regard to my self, my family, my community and the world at large.

Do I have faith that collectively we can solve the challenges we face?

Do I have faith that the world we experience is a result of our collective choices and that by changing our choices we can change our world?

Do I have faith in the desire of humanity to live in peace and harmony with the other life forms on this planet?

In my view the question of whether one chooses faith or fear is not really a choice. To choose fear is not life affirming. To choose fear is not life altering. To choose fear catapults me into a life of 'fight or flight' - a world of chaos and suffering. The only real option is faith.

When I was in my time of personal crisis due to the critical medical needs of my son Joshua I sought answers from a wide range of sources. One area I investigated was the religions of the world. I wanted to know what wisdom the various religions had to guide me during my suffering and despair. I noticed that one idea, one directive was proposed over and over again, regardless whether the teacher was Christian, Buddhist, Jew or Muslim. The message was - *"Fear Not"*.

There is no value in fear. Fear causes contraction, paralysis, flight or fight. Fear activates the part of our neurological structure that is called the *'Reptilian Brain'*. This is the oldest part of our brain stem that is concerned only with survival. It responds in a highly reactive and competitive way. There is no capacity within the reptilian brain for reflection, thought, dialogue, compromise, collaboration or creativity.

Given the complexity of the world today it is impossible to solve our challenges using our reptilian brains. Instead we must access our higher brain - that part of the brain where logic, rational thought, intuition, innovation and creativity prevail. Some people call this our Divine self. I believe that we are our most 'divine' when we respond to the world as *'creative'* beings rather than *'reactive'* beings.

What will you choose - faith or fear?

Creating Watermelons

Last week my family and I enjoyed a beautiful summer's evening by indulging in a ripe red watermelon. In addition to the joy of being refreshed by this beautiful fruit, I was reminded of a powerful memory from childhood.

When I was nine years old my mother cut up some watermelon for my siblings and I to enjoy. At that time watermelon had seeds that needed to be separated from the fruit of the melon. After consuming a number of slices I had a nice little pile of dark watermelon seeds.

Looking at the seeds my nine-year-old mind was inspired with the idea of planting the seeds and growing my own watermelon. This would allow me to enjoy watermelon whenever I chose. I rushed outside and buried the seeds in the middle of my mother's rose garden. Day after day I tended to those seeds, watering them carefully and delighting when green shoots began to emerge.

Over the course of a few weeks the tender shoots grew into large broad leaves, which easily engulfed the adjacent roses. While I took immense pride in my creation my mother lamented at how her roses were being buried under a jungle of watermelon leaves.

One Saturday morning my mother woke me bright and early. With great excitement she announced that my watermelon plant had produced its first melon.

Hurriedly I pulled on some shorts and ran barefoot and bare-chested down the stairs to witness this miracle first hand. There nestled in amongst the leaves of the watermelon plant lay a huge green melon. I hoisted the melon into my arms and proudly marched around the yard.

The joy of the day was captured on film. The image shows a proud nine year old positioned next to his melon with a grin as large as the melon. This was a proud moment in the life of a nine year old. It was an image that sat in a frame on the top of my dresser for years as a reminder of my power to create.

Fast-forward thirty years. At a family gathering I reminisced about my beautiful watermelon. I shared with the others my pride at my accomplishment.

My mother, overhearing my telling of the story remarked, *"You know that you didn't grow that watermelon."* *"Of course I did. Don't you remember?"* I exclaimed. *"Oh, I remember."* she said. *"I remember how that watermelon plant of yours had taken over my rose garden."*

"I figured the only way to end this was to buy a watermelon and place it next to your plant. Don't you recall that the watermelon wasn't attached to the plant?"

The words of my mother filled me with shock and confusion. I began to feel anger and resentment rise in me. Anger that my long held story of having grown a beautiful watermelon was a fiction, and resentment at being deceived by my own mother.

For years I carried the story of the watermelon as a symbolic gesture of my ability to create in the world. To be informed that I had not created the watermelon was hard to accept. My watermelon story was now tainted with disappointment and hurt. I stuck the photo of the nine year old with his watermelon in the bottom of my drawer.

Recently I was reminded of my watermelon story. I reflected more upon this experience. To my surprise I discovered an even deeper message in this event. I concluded that I <u>had</u> created the watermelon after all. While the melon didn't manifest as I thought, a melon did manifest.

I again use the watermelon story to remind myself that I am a powerful and creative being. I also use the story to remind me that the manifestation of my intention may not always emerge as I expect. Sometimes life provides its gifts in ways other than I anticipate.

I've since learned that the creative process involves declaring my intentions and then surrendering and allowing life to support my intentions in anyway that is good for all concerned. I did create a watermelon. It was through the wisdom and generosity of my loving mother! And she got her rose garden back. That picture of the nine year old grinning from ear to ear is back on my dresser.

Suffering is simply the feedback mechanism of life choices.

~ Gregg Braden
Walking Between the Worlds
The Science of Compassion

Suffering Is Optional

In 2007 my family and I stepped into an exotic adventure. We made the decision to climb Mount Kilimanjaro in Tanzania, Africa. Mount Kilimanjaro is the seventh highest peak on the planet with an elevation of more than 19,000 feet.

In more ways than anticipated the climb was the journey of a lifetime. Success on the journey required stamina, persistence, intention and acceptance. Through the first two days of the climb all I could do was keep my head down and my eyes focused on the heals in front of me due to the dizzying effects of altitude sickness. By day three I had acclimatized to the diminished oxygen to enjoy the views before me.

After five days of climbing we reached the final camp at the base of the summit. Our plan was to begin the ascent at midnight with the goal to peak by 8:00 AM. The climb began in darkness. Our only illumination was a solitary headlamp and the stars that enveloped us.

The temperature hovered around - 20 Celsius. Because of the steepness of the slope we needed to traverse sideways across the mountain face. With half the oxygen available at sea level our lungs and muscles strained with every step. To compound the challenge the slope was covered in loose shale. Every step upward was partially negated by the downward slide of the shale. The pace was painfully slow and difficult.

Upward we carried ourselves paced by the mantra - *"slowly, slowly"*.

About two hours short of the crater's rim I was unable to continue. The cold, altitude sickness, and physical exhaustion had taken their toll. The dream to summit Kilimanjaro was beyond my capacity. After five days of climbing it was necessary to turn around and descend.

It would be easy to interpret this experience as defeat and to see my inability to summit as failure. And yet I felt a huge sense of relief. I had participated in a very powerful experience that invited me to be physically active and intensely present. I shared precious moments with my wife and two of my children. I joined with strangers in a powerful sense of community that comes from facing adversity together. And I discovered an important lesson for myself.

As I stood on the steep slope, fatigued to exhaustion, chilled beyond belief, overcome with nausea and dizziness, I came to an important conclusion - *I had suffered enough*. This realization has served me far beyond the slopes of Kilimanjaro. Through this experience of intense physical suffering I came to realize how suffering has been a constant companion in my life. How I have accepted suffering as a fact of life, even embraced suffering as noble. But now I was done with suffering.

This experience assisted me in recognizing how much of my suffering is *self* created. I now recognize that I have made decisions, held onto beliefs, and maintained courses of action regardless of the suffering I experienced. I did this because of a belief that *suffering was necessary*. During that morning on the side of Mount Kilimanjaro something changed in my psyche. I released the need to suffer.

Now when I experience suffering I pause and examine my suffering:

> *Is my suffering associated with my resistance to reality?*
> If so I move into acceptance.
>
> *Is my suffering the result of having judgment?*
> Yes? Release judgment.
>
> *Am I suffering as a result of telling myself negative stories about what might happen in my future?*
> Change my story.
>
> *Is my suffering a consequence of maintaining a course that no longer serves me?*
> Choose again.

I recall my epiphany from Kilimanjaro and I choose not to suffer. I release the thoughts, actions and beliefs that hold the suffering to me. I choose to end the suffering. I choose another path.

This doesn't mean that I step away from any course of action that is challenging. What it means is that, whatever path I choose, I no longer need to walk in suffering. I can walk the path with ease and grace and with peace and joy regardless of the challenge. And I am open to the possibility that the suffering is an indication I may be walking a wrong path and may need to choose again.

If you could see what I see, you'd lose your breath for sure.
You are the perfect replications and the ones that I adore.
I carved you from a diamond and polished you with love
Then I sent you out beyond the veil
so you might choose the love.

Oh my sweet creations your beauty makes me weep
Oh my sweet creations the whole world's at your feet
And one day soon you'll see it.

~ Denise Hagan
Perfect Replications

I Surrender

Of the many essays I have written over the past two years none has elicited as much response as my recent account of my journey climbing Mount Kilimanjaro. I wrote, "*As I stood on the steep slope, fatigued to exhaustion, chilled beyond belief, overcome with nausea and dizziness, I came to an important conclusion - I had suffered enough.*"

Those words resonated with many people. I received numerous emails and messages from individuals who benefited from the realization that each of us creates our suffering by the thoughts and expectations we hold that are out of alignment with reality.

Spiritual teacher Eckhart Tolle writes about the importance of suffering in his book, **The Power of Now** (1997). Tolle describes how suffering is often the path through which we come to our enlightenment. Tolle uses the Christian expression, "*the way of the cross*" to describe individuals who found God through their deep suffering. Tolle explains however that, "*strictly speaking they did not find God through their suffering, rather, they found God through surrender - through total acceptance of what is, into which they were forced by their intense suffering.*"

I've learned that suffering can be valuable. It is through intense pain and suffering that many of us overcome our resistance to what is and arrive at a place of surrender and acceptance.

Tolle explains that the worst thing in your life, your *"cross"*, can become the best thing to happen to you by forcing you into surrender. You surrender because you can't stand the pain of suffering anymore. What happened to me on the slopes of Kilimanjaro was surrender as a result of intense suffering.

I also experienced surrender 20 years ago when my resistance to my son's disabilities and fragile medical condition caused such deep suffering that I could no longer continue down the same path. I was forced into acceptance that my son was disabled and he might die at any moment.

This surrender allowed me to relinquish my attachment to my stories of how my son's life *should have been* and enabled me to make peace with *what is*. The surrender allowed me to fall in love with the son *I have* rather than the son *I don't have*.

Tolle suggests that until recently suffering was the only path to enlightenment. In our state of unconsciousness it was only through intense suffering that we could realize our resistance to reality and chose again.

The good news, according to Tolle, is there are an increasing number of humans today whose consciousness is sufficiently evolved to no longer need intense suffering before they realize enlightenment. They don't need to experience years of pain and agony in order to reach peace and joy. All that is required is the willingness to accept *responsibility for their suffering* and *choose to end the suffering*.

In my seminars I regularly invite participants to play with the idea they are one hundred percent responsible for their thoughts, feelings and behaviors. This includes their suffering. This means they can no longer say, *"You make me happy"* or *"You made me angry"*.

Taking one hundred percent responsibility means accepting that "*I make me happy*" and "*I make me angry*".

At a recent speaking engagement a gentleman approached me after my presentation. He shared with me that he and his wife heard me speak on a previous occasion about taking one hundred percent responsibility. His initial reaction was that I was one hundred percent full of nonsense.

After hearing my presentation, however, his wife suggested they experiment with this idea of taking one hundred percent responsibility. He admitted these last two years have been the best years of his life. He now realizes that the way he had been living previously - projecting responsibility for his thoughts, feelings and behaviors onto others was the nonsense.

Are you ready to end your suffering?

Are you willing to take one hundred percent responsibility for creating your suffering?

Are you ready to choose peace and joy regardless of what life offers?

If not, what are you resisting?

What if you surrendered and accepted?

Are you ready to set down your cross?

I hope so, because you deserve to experience abundant peace and joy.

*. . . if the two (thought and feeling) make peace
with each other in this one house (the body),
they will say to the mountain, 'Move away,'
and it will move away.*

~ Adapted from the Nag Hammadi Library

Responding to Change

We are entering a new era. After years of steady and predictable growth we appear to be in a time of substantial change. The health of the world's financial institutions are no longer as robust as they once were. Companies like **General Motors** that formed the foundation of our modern society are at risk of foreclosure.

Even our housing market, which has witnessed phenomenal growth in both value and number of units built, is in a time of stagnation and regression. Much of what we relied on for our wealth and security no longer seems as solid and secure as it once was.

How we respond to the unpredictability of change is key to our happiness and future success. It is not uncommon to respond to change with fear and trepidation. Many respond to the change by resisting the change. A better response might be to identify strategies to enable us to move through change with grace and ease rather than fear and resentment.

Below are a number of ideas and strategies that might assist us in moving through this period of change more successfully:

1. **Accept the change**.

Resisting the change will not alter the course or the speed of change. It will however alter us into individuals who are angry and resentful.

Successful people not only accept the change they embrace the change. They see change as an *ally* rather than an *adversary*. Change can be a *catalyst* for growth and innovation. It can create the openings and opportunities needed to enable us to re-create our life and our society in better and healthier ways.

2.   **Participate in the change process**.

Research informs us that those who participate as an *active* agent in change are healthier and happier than those who sit back and wait for others to decide how to respond to the change.

Look for ways you can participate in creating new ideas and actions during this time of transformation. Look for opportunities to use the transformational power of change to create a better world. Become a 'creator' rather than a 'reactor'.

3.   **Look Where You Want to Go.**

Look for the openings that change provides. A number of years ago I worked with an individual who was involved in professional racing. This individual shared with me what racecar drivers do in the event their car goes out of control. He explained the driver "*looks for an opening in the field of cars*". By doing so the car moves *toward* the opening.

Most people look at the walls or obstacles. By doing so they move toward the walls or drive into the obstacles. His advice is to "*look where you want to go*".

4.   **Be positive.**

We can do this!

Henry Ford understood - *"Those who think they can and those who think they can't are both right."*

Focus on changing your reaction to change. How you respond to change is key to your success. Viktor Frankl, author of **Man's Search for Meaning** (1988) states –

> *"When we are no longer able to change a situation, we are challenged to change ourselves."*

Move into the change with optimism.

5. **Build collaborative relationships.**

Research indicates that what keeps people safe is dependent upon the number of relationships a person has. The greater the number of relationships, the safer an individual is. The fewer relationships, the more vulnerable the individual is. During times of upheaval and uncertainty it is important to invest time and energy in building relationships.

Every successful business knows that innovation is essential to its survival. They also know that the more individuals who participate in generating solutions the more likely a successful outcome will be achieved. A group's IQ is higher than an individual's IQ.

As I enter into this time of change and uncertainty I follow the advice shared on a bumper sticker. It stated –

> *The best way to predict the future is to create it.*

What lies behind us and what lies before us
are small matters compared to what lies within us.

~ Ralph Waldo Emerson

Secrets to a Peaceful Mind

I didn't always have a peaceful mind. For much of my adult life my mind was in a constant state of turmoil. Those voices in my head chattered away non-stop. Even sleep seemed to have little impact in slowing my mind's activity. All of this activity kept me occupied and exhausted.

Two powerful ideas encouraged me to develop a quiet mind. The first idea is that the physical body doesn't distinguish between a 'real' event and an 'imagined' event. Therefore events that only exist in my imagination can and do have the same physical and emotional consequences as real events. The second idea was the discovery that most people think more negative thoughts than positive thoughts - about nine times as many negative thoughts as positive thoughts.

As I began to monitor my own thoughts I discovered I had an even higher percentage of negative thoughts to positive thoughts. This intense negative thinking created all of my suffering. I finally decided that I had suffered enough. I committed myself to quieting my mind and becoming a peaceful person. The challenge was - how? How does one quiet a mind that has run incessantly for years or even decades?

Eckhart Tolle, author of **The Power of Now** offers valuable insight into the taming of the human mind. He invites us to notice *where* we are living. *Are we living in the past, the present, or the future?*

I noticed that I spent very little time in the present. Most of my life was about *remembering* the past or *imagining* the future. According to Tolle life only exists in the present. The rest is an illusion. Most of us live in the illusion. We live with the idea that the next moment will be better or worse than this moment. Unfortunately, living in the illusion causes us to miss out on *this* moment and eventually to miss out on life.

Tolle also invites us to *witness* ourselves. He encourages us to stand back mentally and notice our self as we engage in life. He then asks a simple question. *Who is the real you? Is it the one involved in the drama or the one noticing the drama?*

I've learned to notice myself as I interact with others. Much of what I notice is pretty entertaining! It's like having a front row seat at a play. I've learned to laugh at myself. I've also learned not to take my self and my life so seriously.

I've learned that regardless of the circumstances I'm in, they will pass. Life is in constant change. Whenever I'm involved in some drama I simply remind myself, "*This too shall pass*". I've also learned that no matter how challenging life is I can always manage *this* moment. I can manage whatever is occurring *now*. What I can't manage is my imagining of what *might* happen. The reason I can't manage my imagining is because it doesn't really exist. My imaginings are simply *made up stories* that only exist in my head.

The secret to a peaceful mind is rather simple - *live in the present*. Allow myself to be in this moment. Be in one place at a time - this place. Finally, I've learned that '*being*' is more important than '*doing*'. We are human *beings* not human *doings*. My way of *being* in this moment is more important than what I *do* in this moment. And so I choose to be peaceful, joyful, grateful and accepting regardless of whatever is occurring in this moment.

Something Must Be Done

A friend who heard me speak on the need for peace challenged me on my position of peaceful co-existence. *"Something must be done"*, he declared. *"What would you do with these terrorists, these radicals who only wish us dead?"*

My difficulty with his question is that I don't construct the world this way. I don't see others as *'radicals, terrorists, or insurgents'*. I see them as like me. I see them as wanting what I want, needing what I need - peace, joy, dignity, respect, food, shelter, and security. I see them as mothers and fathers, brothers and sisters, neighbors and friends. When I view them this way I am unable to see war and killing as the solution to our dilemma of peaceful co-existence.

And so in response to my friend's genuine search for an alternative way my response is simply this - *change our language.*

I believe language is very powerful. Language has the capacity to frame our perspective. It creates the lens through which we view the world and determines how we make meaning of our experiences. I notice that when war is being promoted the language changes such that we no longer see the other as a human being, a loved one, someone worthy of honor and respect. Instead we dehumanize them. We use language that demonizes and makes them unlike us.

The first battle to ending war is to employ language that honors all of us. When the question is asked – *What should we do?* this is a good place to start.

*Responsibility does not only lie with the leaders of our
countries or with those who have been appointed
or elected to do a particular job.
It lies with each of us individually.*

*Peace starts within each one of us.
When we have inner peace,
we can be at peace with those around us.*

~ Dalai Lama

Cultivating Happiness

How does one cultivate happiness? It is easy to be happy when life matches our desires and expectations. But how does one maintain happiness in the face of adversity? How does one create peace and joy in the midst of anger and fear?

In my quest to find peace, joy and happiness one of my most valuable teachers has been His Holiness, the Dalai Lama. I attended a lecture on **Cultivating Happiness** when the Dali Lama visited Vancouver a couple of years ago. I benefited from the wisdom of this remarkable individual who has learned the secrets to happiness.

His success is impressive given the Dalai Lama has been in forced exile from his country, home and people for all of his adult life. If anyone has justification to be angry, hurt, resentful or retaliatory the Dalai Lama has more than enough reason.

Yet, the Dalai Lama does not carry resentment. He does not hold hatred. He does not condemn. He does not advocate for war. Instead he speaks of compassion and peace.

When asked if the use of force is warranted to remove the occupying Chinese military from Tibet the Dalai Lama replied, "*Why would I advocate aggression against the Chinese? They are my brothers and sisters. They just don't know it yet.*"

How do we cultivate happiness? How do we create peace? How do we develop harmony on the planet?

The current wisdom is to use force to create peace. The Dalai Lama offers another solution - *"Recognize others as human beings. Treat them as your brothers and sisters. Acknowledge that mentally, emotionally, and physically we are all the same."*

He explains, *"Wars occur because we mentally divide the world into 'us' and 'them'. Force is no way to deal with differences. Differences will always exist."* The secret to peace and harmony is to recognize the similarities. Success in relationships occurs when we find common ground.

The Dalai Lama listed the many wars that have occurred in the last century and are occurring now. He described this as *"the century of destruction"*. Then he invited each of us to participate in a new century - *"a century of dialogue"*.

"The use of force is out of date", he declares. *"You cannot promote human values through force."*

So, what might this look like? What steps ought we take to move toward a peaceful world?

The Dalai Lama's advice is simple - *"Educate the heart. Create peace through inner peace"*. A calm mind is essential to deal with complex issues. Address the world's issues from a calm mind, not a reactive one.

Secondly, narrow the gap between the rich and the poor. The Dalai Lama informs us that the large gap between those that have and those that have not is not only *morally* wrong it is *practically* wrong as well. You will never create peace in the world when your brother or sister is without food, shelter, clean drinking water and dignity.

Some might dismiss the Dalai Lama's message as naïve, overly optimistic, even foolish. Yet something must be done. It's clear that the current method is not working. It is self evident that polarizing the world into 'us' and 'them', 'heroes' and 'villains' does not work.

Our governments have spent trillions of dollars on their current strategy of using force to solve our differences. Many of us use force to solve differences in our personal lives at home and work. We impose our solution rather than create solutions together through dialogue as equal partners.

It's time we experimented with a new strategy. It's time we tried the solution offered by the Dalai Lama. It's time we *educated the heart* and recognized the humanity in each and every one.

It's time we experimented with dropping *food* rather than bombs; exchanged *ideas* rather than insults; increased *access* to water, food and medicine rather than imposed sanctions to limit the necessities of life; and opened up *dialogue* rather than silenced others.

Its time we realized we are all are brothers and sisters.

*It is possible that the next Buddha
will not take the form of an individual.
The next Buddha may take the form
of a community -
a community practicing understanding and loving
kindness,
a community practicing mindful living.
This may be the most important thing we do for
the survival of the earth.*

~ Thich Nhat Hanh

Electing Ideas, Not People

Imagine if we used the electoral process as an opportunity to *create*. Imagine if we looked to elections as a time to *share* our dreams, to *define* our core assumptions, to *identify* possibilities, and to be *inspired* by the kind of country and community we might become.

Imagine if we used the electoral process to have leaders *listen* rather than tell, to *engage* citizens in legitimate dialogue to discover what is important to us rather than tell us what is important.

Imagine if the electoral process was an *opportunity for choosing which ideas and dreams* were the most inspirational.

Elections could be such a wonderful opportunity to revitalize our communities, refresh our ideas and cast new visions. They could be a time to brainstorm, to be creative and innovative as we attempt to address the complexities of living in community.

In the upcoming election I'm looking for candidates who recognize the need for change. Our earth, our communities, our homeless neighbors, and our future depends on change happening.

I'm hoping for candidates clear enough to articulate their dreams, assumptions and intentions. I'm desiring candidates who are courageous enough to engage in meaningful dialogue with others, especially those of divergent perspectives.

I want candidates who are willing to evaluate their strategies and ask the question, *"Is what we are doing working?"* I want candidates committed to pursuing peaceful ends through peaceful means.

I want us to come together as a community during election time to collectively declare our dreams. I want us to better understand our challenges, opportunities, and each other.

I want us to be inspired by a vision and to find ways we can all participate in that vision.

Imagine that!

During times of universal deceit,
telling the truth becomes a
revolutionary act.

~ George Orwell, 1984

Some Assembly Required

When my daughter Lani was young her most prized possession was a Cabbage Patch doll. Lani needed a Cabbage Patch stroller to proudly display her doll. And so on her next birthday I purchased the focus of her desire.

The stroller came in a box much too small to contain a stroller. I read the fine print on the side - "*Some assembly required*". I struggled for hours to assemble the numerous pieces in a manner that resembled a stroller. Eventually I had something that moved on four wheels with enough parts left over to build something else!

I reflect upon my stroller assembly experience when looking for how we can come together as human beings to share land, resources, space and time. The words - "*some assembly required*" rang in my ears.

Building a healthy community does not happen by accident. It requires intention, thoughtful actions, patience, consideration, and acceptance of values and perspectives different than our own. When we venture boldly into this endeavor we can create a world of comfort, safety, and companionship.

Many years ago I participated in the creation of '**Salal'**, a cooperative housing development in Port Moody, B.C. In the beginning, a housing community based on cooperation and inclusion was just an idea in our imaginations and the land was untouched forest. I remember tramping through the woods, stepping over logs and moving branches to get a glimpse of where my new home might be.

What I remember most was the experience of coming together with a group of people and imagining, designing and considering the dreams and wishes of the many families who would share this space and call it home.

The result was a beautiful interplay of trees and earth, bricks and mortar to create a place where people could live. The goal was to create a community where people would come together and share life. The design included a common room for community gatherings, a number of playground areas for children of all ages, level walkways for mothers and fathers with strollers, special design considerations for individuals with mobility challenges, and the preservation of the most majestic trees on the site.

The design decision that made the most impact was the idea to locate the parking area adjacent to the street. This allowed for as much green space as possible, and more importantly, invited people out of their cars. This simple decision created daily opportunities for individuals to interact with their neighbors. I remember many an evening where the three-minute walk from my car to my front door took 30 minutes as I engaged in rich conversations along the way.

A healthy and peaceful community doesn't happen on it's own. It requires the thoughtful actions and intentions of committed citizens who behave in ways to ensure that we live in a safe and healthy community.

A healthy and peaceful world doesn't happen on it's own either. It requires the thoughtful actions and intentions of committed citizens who behave in ways to ensure that everyone lives in safe and healthy communities regardless of race, religion, nationality or resources. In both cases some assembly is required.

Responding to Loss

Denise came to see me shortly after her fiancé had been killed in a motor vehicle accident. The driver of the other vehicle had been drinking and was legally impaired at the time of the accident. The death of her fiancé occurred just weeks prior to her wedding day.

Denise was understandably angry, resentful and sad. During the first forty-five minutes of her time with me she expressed an intense outpouring of emotions. She expressed anger. She shared her sadness and grief. She was immersed in fear. And she even talked of revenge. Eventually Denise released the deep well of emotions that had built up inside her and this allowed a moment of silence.

I interrupted the silence with a question. *"Denise,"* I asked her, *"If we could speak with your fiancé, wherever he is, and ask what he would wish for you now, what do you think his answer would be?"*

After a moment of reflection a smile came to Denise's face. *"I know what Gary would wish for me."* she responded. *"Gary would want me to be happy. He would want me to claim my joy and get on with living my life fully."*

"I think you're right." I replied. *"I suspect Gary would wish with all his heart that you not stay in anger, fear or resentment, and instead that you embrace peace and joy; that you continue to live the happiness the two of you shared."*

I then added a suggestion for her consideration. *"Denise, I wonder if a way to honor your fiancé would be to wake each day and fill your heart with peace and joy and live this way as a means of honoring Gary."*

I could see that Denise embraced my suggestion. Her face filled with joy as she grinned from ear to ear. *"I'll do that she said."* There was little more for me to say. I gave Denise a hug and off she went.

One month later Denise returned. *"I'm doing really well"* she declared. *"Every day when I wake up I consciously hold Gary in my heart and I make a commitment to living the day peacefully and joyfully."*

"My problem" she continued, *"is my parents and Gary's parents don't understand my joy. They think I must not have loved Gary. They think if you love someone, you should be angry when they die. I've asked them to see you Ted, but they don't want to let go of their anger and sadness."*

I acknowledged Denise's challenge. I have seen this many times before. Many of us have been socialized to tell ourselves stories that undermine our ability to live in peace and joy. And so we live a life filled with anger, fear and resentment, not knowing that the solution is within us.

We are wise to recognize the kind of stories we tell ourselves. Mastering our stories is the key to our happiness. The power of storytelling was so clearly understood by the Hopi that they declared - *"He who tells the stories rules the world."*

How The World is Changed

There is a growing consciousness that using force to create peace does not achieve the desired result. Yet knowing what *not* to do does not guide us in how to respond to discord in a positive and peaceful way. *What peace-making strategies might move us from divided and combative positions to positions of mutual trust and support?*

Authors Francis Westley, Brenda Zimmerman, and Michael Patton chronicle numerous innovative strategies in their book, **Getting to Maybe. How the World Is Changed**. (Random House, 2006). Their book contains amazing stories of personal and community transformation to inspire us that a different world is possible.

One of their tales instructive to our desire to create a more peaceful world is the story of Jeff Brown. Brown is a minister in Boston's inner city, an area known for homicides, violence, and gang warfare. Brown would regularly preach sermons about the unacceptability of violence, yet in spite of his preaching things remained the same. Reverend Brown's sermons were clearly not making a difference.

After dialoguing with fellow ministers Brown and others decided to form a 'street committee'. Their goal was to go out on to the streets of Boston and connect with the young gang members. Every Friday from midnight to 4:00 AM the members of the street committee gathered in the inner city neighborhoods and walked around.

The initial street walks were frightening. This was a world Brown had made every effort to avoid.

After weeks of walking and observing the youth gangs from a distance Brown reported that something shifted. The ministers saw that each gang was like a family and that the members were creating and defending their families. This shift in perception opened up the possibility of communicating with the gang members.

Within weeks the adults of the street committee were engaged in rich discussions with the youth to understand *their* world and *their* experience. The result was a spectacular decline in violence. The change was so spectacular the New York Times described the event as the *'Boston Miracle'*.

What did Reverend Brown and the others do? They changed the way they acted and thought.

Brown now recognizes that he had been living by a set of rules and assumptions given to him by his culture that impeded his ability to solve this situation. He describes three rules that resulted in behaviors, which only reinforced the violence:

1. The Rule of Separation
There is a difference between the gang and the rest of us.

2. The Rule of Avoidance
The gangs are dangerous and should be avoided.

3. The Rule of Intolerance
Condemn their violence and make no effort to understand it.

Through the innovative and courageous actions of the street committee the priests and gang members began to connect with one another.

With this connection they reevaluated their assumptions about each other. They discovered they were more *alike* than they were *different*. They discovered they held the same values - loyalty, respect, safety, dignity and quality of life. They discovered they could work through the challenges of their circumstances in a peaceful and respectful way.

We can learn from Reverend Brown and his colleagues. This story offers us hope in our efforts to resolve conflict in a peaceful way, whether it occurs in our individual worlds of family, colleagues and community, or on the world stage between Nations.

When we challenge our core assumptions, when we open up to behaving in different ways, when we seek to understand and accept, miracles can and will happen.

Where in your world do you hold assumptions and practice behaviors that reinforce the rules of separation, avoidance, and intolerance?

Are you courageous and committed enough to try something new?

This is how the world is changed.

When you solve a problem through force
you plant seeds for another problem.

~ Dalai Lama

Beyond Stubborn

A young woman came to see me this week. Lisa was angry and scared. Lisa was angry at the amount of suffering she was experiencing and scared that nothing would change. Lisa's suffering was as a result of her inability to work through differences with her spouse and family successfully. Differences in opinion, perception or values usually resulted in conflict.

Upon deeper investigation the cause of Lisa's suffering became apparent. Nowhere in her past was Lisa exposed to individuals who modeled collaborative problem solving. No one had taught Lisa the skills of respecting differences and creating win-win solutions. Lisa was taught to win at all costs which often meant making others lose.

Lisa admitted to *"being stubborn"* - to sticking with a position or perception even when she knew it to be incorrect or inaccurate. Lisa diagnosed her situation as caused by 'a stubborn personality'. I didn't buy her story.

No one chooses a position that doesn't work out of pure stubbornness. The truth was Lisa was afraid. Lisa was afraid to be wrong. Life had treated Lisa badly when she was wrong. And so Lisa rarely admitted to being wrong. Instead Lisa learned to make others wrong so that she could be right.

Lisa is not unusual. Most people are suffering. Most are unable to create win-win solutions. It's not for lack of desire or trying. It's for lack of knowing how.

Let's face it. Most of our role models today demonstrate a *competitive* style of living; a style where one wins and the rest lose - whether it's commerce, sports, politics, the legal system, or war.

Consider the game of 'musical chairs'. It is a children's game played almost universally. *What philosophy is this game based on? What skills are encouraged? What experience is being created?*

In my experience I've consistently witnessed the following outcome – one happy winner, and many unhappy losers. Usually the strongest, fastest, and most aggressive child wins, while the gentle and considerate are the first to lose.

"Does this way of living work?" "What are the consequences of viewing life through the lens of win-lose, right-wrong, good-bad?"

The result is a conflicted community, a divided community, and anger and suffering. The state of our world today, with numerous wars occurring simultaneously, is a reflection of our failure to engage in problem solving strategies that honors differences.

In a recent address given by US President George Bush, Bush mocked President hopeful Senator Barack Obama for his willingness to dialogue with Iran, North Korea, Cuba, and other "enemies". Bush called this action "foolish delusion". The world is a reflection of our consciousness at this time.

The good news is that individuals like Lisa are tired of the suffering. They are angry at losing. They want to find another way; a better way. Better ways do exist, however we must be willing to let go of seeing the world through the lens of win-lose. We must identify what it is we are committed to, and then do everything in our power to move in this direction.

Recently I heard an interview on CBC radio with Alan Young. Young is a professor of law at York University's Osgoode Hall and Director of **The Innocence Project** - a program to address the problem of wrongfully convicted individuals.

In the interview Professor Young told of admonishing his students who come to him boasting they had *"won their first case"*. His response was, *"I don't want to hear you say you won. What I want to hear is that justice was served."*

Unfortunately our justice system is similar to the other systems in our society. It is focused on winning and losing rather than on creating justice. Similarly our system of national security produces winners and losers rather than peace. And our political system produces winners and losers rather than good government.

It's time we grew up. It's time we transcended seeing the world in such simple and reductive ways. Its time we found ways where everyone is honored. Its time we stopped being stubborn.

Our future depends on it.

Peace is a matter of application, rather than theory.
One must not be mistaken into thinking that
he or she is contributing to peace on Earth
just because one is thinking and speaking about peace.

Peace is not something that can be realized through
words and thoughts only. Peace can only be realized
through concrete and sustained cultural and
societal efforts at healing the body, mind, and spirit
of yourself, your neighbors, your society,
and the humanity at large.

~ Ilchi Lee, Author
Peaceology

What Keeps People Safe?

What keeps people safe? Conventional wisdom says our safety is dependent upon the number of Police Officers in a community, the size of a Nation's military, or more recently, the use of technology. As a result, whenever the issue of increasing safety is debated the solutions put forward are usually the same - increase policing and military budgets, and install cameras and other sophisticated technology to monitor communication and behavior.

But do these methods work? Do these strategies actually increase our safety and security?

A few years ago research was conducted in the disability community to determine what keeps individuals with a disability safe. The research revealed an interesting phenomenon. Safety is dependent upon the number of *relationships* a person has. The more relationships, the greater an individual's safety. The fewer relationships, the more vulnerable they are.

If this principle applies to large groups just as it does to individuals then communities and nations that want to increase the safety of their citizens will not accomplish this by increasing the size of their police or military or by developing sophisticated technology. The method for creating safer communities is to *build connections between individuals*. Safety comes from building relationships with those who are different, marginalized, or excluded. My friend Jerome Bouvier did just that.

Jerome is the Executive Director of **Access Youth Services Society** (www.accessyouth.org). Access has a mandate to increase the safety and well being of the youth in this community. With the aid of a modified shuttle bus Access staff travel to areas of the community where youth naturally congregate – convenience stores, parks, schools, etc.

Their primary service is **Project REACH OUT**. The goal of Project REACH OUT is to *reach out* to youth and build relationships. The idea is through these relationships the safety and security of youth increases.

Access has witnessed a significant shift in the perceptions and attitudes of the youth with whom they have established a relationship on a first name basis. By reaching out to youth the youth acquire the perception that they are valued, that adults in the community care about their well-being, and that they are welcome and included regardless of the color of their hair, the kind of clothes they wear, their nationality, sexual orientation, religion or intelligence. The result is youth take better care of themselves, feel safer and more secure, and have a greater sense of belonging.

One of the additional benefits of this strategy is that it doesn't require significant *financial* resources. What is required is *human* resources. Resources as - caring and compassion, a willingness to reach out to others, a desire to understand those who are different, and a commitment to honor the rights, gifts and contributions of all individuals.

I wonder what kind of world we might have if more communities had 'reach out projects'; if more people talked to strangers; if more governments invested resources in building connections with their 'enemies'; if we built bridges rather than walls between cultures, races, religions and nations. Let's make this world a better place. We have the resources - it is within each of us.

———

How Martin Luther King Revolutionized America

When Martin Luther King was responding to the civil rights crisis in the United States in the 1960's he had his fellow activists agree to the following:

MEDITATE daily.

REMEMBER always that the nonviolent movement seeks *justice* and *reconciliation* - not victory.

WALK and **TALK** in the manner of *love*.

PRAY daily in order that *all* men might be free.

SACRIFICE *personal* wishes in order that all men might be free.

OBSERVE with both friend and foe the ordinary rules of courtesy.

SEEK to perform regular service for others and the world.

REFRAIN from the violence of fist, tongue, or heart.

STRIVE to be in good spiritual and bodily health.

FOLLOW the directions of the movement.

Do not ask for change.
Be the change.

~ Gandhi

Who Is Responsible for Peace?

The festive season is upon us. At this time of year, more than any other, we yearn for peace. Our singers sing songs of peace. Our greetings invite peace. Yet the peace we so desperately yearn for often elude us.

Newspapers are filled with stories of anger and fear. Televisions broadcast pictures of war, despair and destruction. *What it is that prevents us from experiencing peace in our world, our cities, our homes, and our hearts? Why is it that the peace we so desperately desire is so rarely experienced?*

Maybe a better question is - *"Who is responsible for peace?" "Who is responsible for creating a peaceful world?"*

My own journey to experience peace revealed how little I knew about creating peace. For much of my life I held the assumption that peace would come *from* others. That peace would occur when world leaders chose peace rather than war.

As a consequence my responsibility for creating peace was little more than that of an impatient bystander or a vocal cheerleader. Years of living without peace, however, made painfully clear that this path to peace was an illusion; that my strategy of how to experience peace was flawed.

I now know if I am to experience peace then it will need to come from me; that it will be the result of *my* efforts rather than the efforts of *others*. I am responsible for the peace I cherish. If peace is to occur I must create this peace with in me first.

It is impossible to create peace in the world if I do not come from a place of peace. Peace begins with me. Gandhi said it clearest - **Be the change you want the world to be**. Peace, joy, and happiness are my responsibility.

But what does this mean? How is the experience of peace my responsibility?

The fact is that my emotional state is a direct consequence of my mental state. Happiness and sadness, trust and fear, hope and despair are all created in my mind by the kind of story I tell myself or by the stories I allow to be told to me.

My experience of life is determined by the *meaning* I assign to life. If I want to experience peace then it is my responsibility to take charge of the meanings that I assign; take charge of the stories I tell myself and allow to be told to me.

I now realize how little responsibility I took for the stories I told myself. I often accepted, without reservation or reflection, the stories imparted by others. The result was I was never in charge of my mental and emotional body. What I thought and felt was in the hands of others. No wonder I rarely experienced peace!

I am now clear why peace eluded me. It is because I acted as though I was not responsible for creating peace. I acted as if I was powerless. I let others determine my perceptions and perspectives. *I was asleep.*

If I want to experience peace I need to take responsibility for creating peace. I need to claim my power as a storyteller. I need to monitor the stories I tell myself.

I need to be vigilant in telling stories of compassion and understanding, of respect and dignity, and of the right of all species to live in harmony rather than stories of fear and scarcity, of us against them, or of the superiority of one race, one nation, or one species over another.

A native tale beautifully captures the secret of peaceful living. In the story an elder is walking with his grandson. After a while the grandfather interrupts the silence and declares, *"Grandson, there are two wolves fighting in my heart. One wolf is angry and vindictive and wants to hurt others. The other wolf is kind, compassionate, and loving."*

The grandson, hearing the words of his grandfather is filled with fear and anxiety. *"Which wolf will win the battle of your heart?"* asks the grandson.

The wise elder replies, *"My heart will be won by the wolf that wins the battle of every man's heart. It will be the wolf that I feed."*

Which wolf do you feed?

People are like stained glass windows.
They sparkle and shine when the sun is out,
but when the darkness sets in,
their true beauty is revealed only if there
is a light from within.

~ Elisbeth Kubler-Ross

About the Author

Ted Kuntz is a father, husband, and citizen. He is also an author and a psychotherapist in private practice. Ted lives in Vancouver, Canada.

Ted is passionate about his community and has invested countless hours in supporting various organizations whose common mission is to improve the quality of life of the community and the individuals who reside there.

Ted is the author of **Peace Begins With Me**. This book captures his personal journey as the father of a disabled child. This deeply personal story is an inspiration to all of us who want to move past pain and anger and claim peace and joy.

Ted is also the co-author of **8 Weeks to A Better Relationship**. This book contains much of the wisdom Ted acquired from his twenty-five years as a psychotherapist assisting individuals to improve their lives and relationships.

Ted is highly pursued to share his stories and present his wisdom to a wide variety of audiences from social services to the corporate world. Ted's passion is to create a peaceful world where we all belong.

To contact Ted Kuntz:

Email: **tedjkuntz@gmail.com**
Web site: **www.peacebeginswithme.ca**

Additional Products

Peace Begins With Me – Soft Cover

Captures Ted's personal journey of reclaiming his peace and his joy after his son became disabled at five months of age. This internationally acclaimed book is a summary of the wisdom he acquired on this journey. Ted's story is an inspiration to those who are challenged by life and wish to move beyond pain and anger and experience peace and joy.

Peace Begins With Me – DVD

This DVD is a recording of a live presentation on the wisdom contained in Peace Begins With Me. An easy way to share the wisdom of Peace Begins With Me with family, friends, and colleagues.

Total viewing time: 90 minutes.

Peace Begins With Me – e-book

Peace Begins With Me is available for your e-book.

To purchase, please visit
www.peacebeginswithme.ca

Notes, Thoughts, Reflections

Made in the USA
Charleston, SC
26 July 2015